The Courage To Write

62 Devotions to Encourage Your Writing Journey

Compiled and Edited by

Rachel Britton & Lucinda Secrest McDowell

The Courage To Write

Dedicated to everyone who is called to write, and even unsure of their calling. Our prayer is that as you read these devotions from members of our reNEW community, you will receive the courage to share your story and your words.

"... tell what great things God has done for you."
Luke 8:39 NKJV

Contributors

Valerie Acres
Janet Fisher Aronson
Lynne Bauman
Kate Breckinridge
Rachel Britton
Rebecca Brown
Susan Call
Susan Case
Heidi Chiavaroli
Rachael M. Colby
Jeanne Doyon
Jennifer Drummond
Lorri Dudley
Cynthia Fantasia
Robin Farnsworth
Kim Findlay
Patricia Frost
Desiree Future
Tammy Gerhard
Stephanie Goddard
Cathy Gohlke
Deb Haggerty
Lauri Hawley
Lisa Larsen Hill
Sheryl Holmes
Carla B. Howard
Christa Hutchins
Myra Ingargiola
Clarice James
Tamson Jensen
Carol Kent

Julie Kieras
Kathy Kim
Maureen Laub
Katy Lee
Nancy Tupper Ling
Debbie Lowe
Lucinda Secrest McDowell
Meadow Rue Merrill
Maureen Miller
Susan E. Moody
Angela Nichole
Kathleen O'Malley
Yvonne Ortega
Kirsten Panachyda
Shawn Parisi
Christa Parrish
Rachel Paukett
Melissa Pillone
Karen Porter
Jill Robinson
Lori Stanley Roeleveld
Jane Rubietta
Cynthia Ruchti
Cindy Saab
Melanie Shull
Brenna Kate Simonds
Nancy Smith
Renee Story
Konnie Viner
Catrina Welch
Tammy Sue Willey

Table of Contents

A Word About the Words

This book was birthed out of the knowledge that it takes courage to write. Yet, it is also grounded in the belief that God gives us strength and direction each step of the way.

The editors of this book are writers and speakers whose writing journeys brought them together to lead reNEW – spiritual retreat for writers & speakers. Our purpose is to encourage Christian communicators in their calling to write and speak.

Each devotion is written by a woman from the reNEW community who stepped out in courage to follow God's calling.

Some of our writers are veteran authors and communicators who have persevered in their calling for decades. You may recognize their names. Each has served as reNEW faculty over the years. Others are new to writing and joined our community to learn skills and find encouragement as they pursue writing and speaking. This book gives them the first opportunity to be in print. Most of the authors are somewhere in between. But each has a unique story of how God has given courage to move forward in His power.

We chose to self-publish rather than find a traditional publisher for this book. This project, end to end, is an example of the curriculum offered at reNEW retreats: writing devotions, self-editing, self-publishing production, marketing, and soul care—all of which are part of a writer's experience in the current publishing climate.

Our hope is these devotions will inspire you to write.

We, as reNEW co-directors, and the reNEW community are with you all the way!

Rachel Britton and Lucinda Secrest McDowell

You Can Do This

Rachel Britton

Have I not commanded you? Be strong and courageous.
Do not be afraid; do not be discouraged,
for the Lord your God will be with you wherever you go.
Joshua 1:9

Black diamonds. Not the kind you find in a ring, but those you discover on ski slopes.

Come with me. I'll take you to the top of one—a "double black"—as they are known. You're standing on the edge where the slope falls sharply away from you. If you move forward, there will be no turning back. Ahead of you, in a blue jacket and matching ski pants, your instructor turns his head and beckons. You hesitate. He waits. Holding your breath, you shuffle towards him on your skis with legs as stiff as a wooden doll. You daren't look down the slope. Instead, you dig the edges of your skis into the soft snow, hoping you won't slide forward. Fear shouts in your ear "you can't do this," drowning out common sense which says your instructor would never take you anywhere you're not capable of skiing.

It can be the same with writing. Fear stops us from moving forward, even though we know God would not lead us anywhere he wouldn't equip us. Fear stops us sharing our stories, even though God is beckoning us to do so.

"Be strong and courageous. Do not be afraid; do not be discouraged."

God spoke these words to Joshua, Moses' aide. Moses had died and God had given Joshua instructions to lead the Israelites across the Jordan and into the land He promised them. God also gave Joshua specific assurances. He would be with Joshua and never leave him. Every place Joshua stepped; he would have success.

Yet, Joshua, a skilled fighter, who had been with Moses when he communed with God, needed to be reminded multiple times to be "strong and courageous." "Have I not commanded you?" God says. In other words, "I've told you before and I am repeating it again." Fear could have made Joshua turn away, but courage made him move forward with God.

The key to Joshua's success was for him to: "Keep this Book of the Law always on your lips; meditate on it day and night, so that you may be careful to do everything written in it" (Joshua 1:8a).

The key to moving forward in our writing is to keep our eyes on God—to spend time with Him and in His Word, and to be obedient to everything He asks of us.

Where is God leading you with your writing? Are you afraid to follow? Step out. Be strong and courageous.

"I can do this." are the words you say to yourself as you turn your skis downhill and follow your instructor. "Lord, with my eyes on you, I can do this," is the prayer you say as you begin to write.

Rachel Britton is an author and speaker, and an avid skier. In the winter, you can often find in the Rocky Mountains either writing voraciously or on the slopes working on overcoming her fear of skiing double black diamonds. RachelBritton.com

When God Chooses Your Readers

Cynthia Ruchti

I was naked, and you gave me clothing. I was sick,
and you cared for me. I was in prison, and you visited me.
Matthew 25:36 NLT

Every author dreams of a spot for his or her books on a particular shelf—Powell's Books in Portland, a large and oft-frequented bookstore in downtown Manhattan, a quaint bookstore in our childhood hometown, in the hands of the person sitting beside us on a plane, on the desk of a talk show host, on a shelf in the writing nook of one of our favorite authors, or on the Jumbotron in Times Square.

I did not imagine that my dream spot would be prison libraries.

I couldn't have pictured that my most treasured reader letters would be from the incarcerated. As my novels or nonfiction were written, my author brain envisioned readers on a train, in a cozy reading corner, bent over a small table at a coffee shop, propped in a pillow-populated bed with a just-right reading light.

How could I have imagined readers pulling a tattered, much-used volume from a library cart wheeled past clanging steel bars by prison guards, or slid off a shelf during open hours in a prison library, or even passed person to person in that clandestine way that is a less "official" delivery method among prisoners?

And how could I have envisioned that it would be the pages of novels where the incarcerated would find hope and courage? Who has that scene in mind when laying fingers to keyboard to write a story?

While these are readers who can't Tweet or post about how much the book meant, they can instead influence others within their tight confines. People I can reach no other way.

A note arrived the other day with a familiar correctional institution postmark and return address. "I struggled reading the book," the prisoner said, "because I'm still emotionally raw. I had to take my time to grieve as I read. But your words gave me such HOPE."

I could claim no ownership to those words.

What blessed that young man were the words that imaginary but true-to-life characters in the novel had communicated: "My first thoughts when waking up are now healthy ones that will set a tone I can draw on instead of being drained by." "I am strong but not self-sufficient." "God is becoming my default thought now, rather than my last resort."

Many hundreds of miles, iron gates, secure locks, and a litany of visitation regulations lay between me and the ability to reach and encourage a prisoner's heart. Or so I thought.

God knows no such barriers, which He's been proving since Old Testament days.

It's not an Instagram-able or Pinterest-worthy image. But I now most long for my books to appear not on the New York Times bestseller list, but in the prison library.

Iron bars are no barrier to hope.

Cynthia Ruchti tells stories hemmed-in-Hope through more than 36 books and through speaking events for women. Her tagline is: I can't unravel. I'm hemmed in Hope. Cynthia is also a literary agent with Books & Such Literary management. CynthiaRuchti.com

Set Apart to Serve

Lynne Bauman

"Before I formed you in the womb I knew you,
before you were born, I set you apart ..."
Jeremiah 1:5

I walked into the room full of women I didn't know. I felt small and insignificant, wondering to myself, "What am I doing at a writer's conference? I don't belong here." All the questions and doubts started running through my mind. It doesn't take much to get us thinking we don't belong or questioning if what we do even matters.

Have you had similar thoughts?

I mustered up a meager dose of courage and tried to reassure myself all would be well. Soon enough I was greeted by a friendly face and met some sweet ladies at my table. By the end of the day, after listening to wonderful inspiring speakers, God reminded me of a truth He revealed to me many years ago.

The memory of that truth felt like an old book that had been covered in dust. I needed to wipe away all the lies that I had allowed to choke out the power of what God had revealed. As I did, the truth of that promise filled my heart again. If felt like being reacquainted with a sweet friend.

The promise? "Before I formed you in the womb I knew you, before you were born, I set you apart ..." (Jeremiah 1:5 NIV). This is what the Lord gently reminded me.

Years ago, this scripture became a life-giving truth for me as it spoke to my worth and value as a daughter of God. Uncovering it again, I found it still spoke to me in the same way. Now, reading it through the lens of a writer gives me the courage to keep going. It reminds me that God has ordained my days—every one! And in doing so, He looks upon me with unfathomable value and worth, and with a specific assignment in mind.

Dear friend, are you struggling to find the courage to write? Are you struggling with the doubts and lies that seem to bombard you at every turn? If so, may I remind you that long before you were a twinkle in your parents' eyes, God placed immeasurable value and worth upon you. He has set you apart for a unique purpose that only you can fulfill. Don't rush past this truth too quickly. I encourage you to sit with it and allow God to speak to your courage-weary heart.

May you know today that God knew you before the foundations of the world. He chose you and set you apart for a special kingdom assignment. Empowered with this truth, may you be filled with God-inspired courage to write. Put pen to paper and allow Him to use you to "bring out the God flavors of this earth!" (Matthew 5:13 MSG).

I'm cheering you on!

Lynne Bauman is a wife, mother, pastor, author, lover of words, and tea drinker. Her joy is found in leading, teaching, and mentoring women. Lynne is Pastor of Women at her church—Walnut Hill Community Church, Bethel, CT. HowGoodIsATimelyWord.wordpress.com

Racing Against Rejection

Heidi Chiavaroli

*Therefore, since we are surrounded by such a great cloud
of witnesses, let us throw off everything that hinders and
the sin that so easily entangles. And let us run with
perseverance the race marked out for us, fixing our eyes on Jesus,
the pioneer and perfecter of faith ...*
Hebrews 12:1-2

I stared at the three offensive numbers on my computer screen, emotion bubbling up in the back of my throat. I hadn't received grades this low since high school calculus. And this was something I actually *liked*. It had taken me weeks to work up the courage to enter the writing contest. I had polished my entry, certain my characters leapt off the page, certain my plot was a page-turning one.

But it was all for nothing. Those numbers shouted the truth: I didn't have what it took to become an author. No wonder I hadn't heard from that agent I queried all those months ago.

I shoved my writing aside for months. Why continue at something I was so pitifully bad at?

But a funny thing happened in those vacant, writing-less months. I kept *longing* to write. God kept pulling me back to the craft of writing. I read somewhere that writing *could* be learned. I clung to this notion. I may not have incredible talent, but I could study and learn. I could persevere. I ran marathons, after all. I knew about training toward a seemingly impossible goal. This time, a writing career would be my race.

I found a critique group, continued to learn the craft, and suffered all manner of rejections until eight years and five manuscripts later, I eventually won the same contest that had depressed me for so many months. This win helped me land a top-notch agent (the agent I never received a response from all those years ago!)

To my dismay, however, rejections continued—this time from publishing houses. I started Manuscript #6. By now, I had put as many hours into writing as a person pursuing their master's degree put into their college education. I refused to see those hours go to waste. (One doesn't run twenty-two miles of a marathon only to quit in the last four miles.) Something *must* simply come from all those writing miles!

I submitted the story, once again gave its fate over to God, and waited.

I will never forget the night my husband and two boys surprised me by coming into the Walmart garden center where I worked. I put down my leaky hose, wiped my hands on my super-attractive blue smock, and hugged them. When my husband told me my agent had left a message on the home phone with news of a contract offer from my dream publishing house, I almost fainted and fell into the petunias—literally.

My dear friends who feel this beautiful pull to write. If you are discouraged or wonder if this dream will ever happen for you, hold fast. Some make it look easy. But for others of us, God has a different timetable, a different plan. Persevere. Throw yourself into the arms of Jesus. And run that race.

———————————

Heidi Chiavaroli is a writer, runner, and grace-clinger. Her debut novel, "Freedom's Ring," was a Carol Award winner and a Christy Award finalist, a Romantic Times Top Pick, and a Booklist Top Ten Romance Debut. Visit her online at HeidiChiavaroli.com

Discover Your Creativity

Carol Kent

*Never doubt God's mighty power to work in you and
accomplish all this. He will achieve infinitely more than your
greatest request, your most unbelievable dream, and exceed
your wildest imagination! He will outdo them all, for
his miraculous power constantly energizes you.*
Ephesians 3:20 TPT

The emcee was exceptionally funny.

I was seated in the audience at a large convention, and the opening ceremonies established a circus theme, complete with clowns, helium balloons, popcorn, and a live elephant. The huge animal thundered down the aisle, causing a major stir on the main floor. Immediately behind him were men in uniform carrying fancy silver-plated shovels.

The emcee adjusted his glasses and calmly stated, "An elephant eats five hundred pounds of food a day and retains only five percent of that amount." The crowd roared with laughter.

That captivating opening set my mind in motion.

Why? It was unexpected, original, clever, hilarious, and intriguing. The entire opening ceremony included the essence of creativity. I was hooked—and then the speaker skillfully reminded us of the volumes of information we take in—and of how little we retain, if we refuse to intentionally act on what we learn.

But what is creativity? It's the use of the imagination or original ideas, especially in the production of an artistic work.

As a speaker and writer, I have discovered six helpful ways to harness creativity for God's purposes:

- Acknowledge the Source of creativity—God Himself. As the Bible says: "In the beginning God created the heavens and the earth" (Genesis 1:1).
- Dare to boldly ask God to pour His creativity into you. Bonnie Emmorey says: "I believe creativity is a gift from God. As Creator of the universe, He has all creativity at His fingertips, and He delights in giving it to us. When I ask Him for it, I'm amazed at the ideas that emerge—not out of my brain, but definitely from Him."
- Allow yourself to be childlike—doodle, daydream, wonder, and explore. Don't schedule every minute so tightly that you can't try something random and new.
- Write regularly in a creativity journal. Include scriptures, pictures, drawings, and phrases that interest you. Sit with your journal 15 minutes a day, even if uninspired.
- Brainstorm with other creative people—regularly and honestly—all ideas can be expressed and discussed.
- Try something new. If it fails, you tried. If it succeeds, it could open great ministry opportunities and adventures.

Thomas Terry and Ryan Lister say: "The rule that should guide your creativity, then, is this: Let everything you create be for God's glory and the world's good ... But do so in a way that you cannot run fast enough to lay your art at the foot of God's throne."

Will you be bold in asking God to pour His creativity into you? With this kind of courage, you can expect results. Try one new thing this week that is out of your comfort zone or your usual routine.

Pray expectantly. Wait with anticipation. Be alert. Tweak the project. Accept wise advice. Give God the glory.

Carol Kent is an international speaker and author of 27 books. She founded the Speak Up Conference, an event to help people develop their speaking and writing skills. Carol also co-founded the non-profit organization, Speak Up for Hope. SpeakUpConference.com

Ask God What to Say

Valerie Acres

Be very careful, then, how you live—
not as unwise but as wise,
Ephesians 5:15

My childhood diaries disappeared. Not recently, in adulthood, but when they were being written—when the expressions were real, raw. Nothing was said. To this day, I have no idea what happened to those pretty books with gold locks and pages filled mostly with anger toward a supposedly loving God who took my mother when I was only seven and toward the stepmother chosen to replace her. For decades, I suspected a family member had taken the diaries and read them.

I lost trust in everyone. I stopped writing.

Has your trust ever been violated in a way that made you shut down self-expression and build barriers so strong that even The Hulk could not break through? Has your confidence ever faltered so severely that you could not expose vulnerability even to someone needing empathy? Have you ever felt isolated amidst the people closest to you and wondered if, possibly, the problem was your inability to connect with them rather than their rejection of you?

Writing seems easy when reading the words of others. But good writing—writing that truly connects with the souls of others—is hard work that takes courage. And self-exposure.

My decision to stop writing was the first of many unwise choices. Rejecting healthy ways to deal with difficult feelings opened the door to some very unhealthy, ungodly ways of doing so: alcoholism, promiscuity, divorce, idolatry of career success, avoidance of intimacy. The list goes on. But God loved me enough to pursue me during forty years of nonsense and to forgive it all.

Through discipline that was less harsh than I deserved, loving encouragement from followers, and an ever-increasing awareness of the Holy Spirit inside me, God drew me back into His family, restored my trust, and inspired me to write again. He loves you just as much!

In Ephesians 5:15, Paul instructs us to be very careful in how we live—"not as unwise but as wise." Being a newcomer to Bible study, my approach in understanding this verse is to read all verses about wisdom. What does wisdom mean? How do we get it? What I learned is this: Wisdom is not knowledge but, rather, the ability to make good use of knowledge. Wisdom and humility go hand-in-hand. Wisdom has an inverse relationship with pride. And, the best way to gain wisdom is to ask God.

Writers, as you decide what to say and to whom, do not be afraid! Ask God. He *will* use scripture, the promptings of the Holy Spirit, and His church, to make your choices wise and help your words reach those who will be blessed to hear them.

Valerie Acres is writer whose passion is welcoming those who feel like outsiders into the Lord's loving family. Valerie left a 20-year career in healthcare advocacy to manage senior housing communities in New England. Her first book is coming soon.

We Are God's Storytellers

Christa Parrish

Each of you should use whatever gift you have received to serve others, as faithful stewards of God's grace in its various forms.
1 Peter 4:10

We are biologically—and spiritually, I would contend—created to interpret the world through stories.

Perhaps this is because our Creator is the ultimate Storyteller. He comes to us not only through His written Word, but in the Living Word. God incarnates His greatest story and allows us to enter into it as both characters and co-authors.

As writers, we all know the power of storytelling, and we've seen that power corrupted.

From the beginning, those who sought to dominate have done so by controlling the stories others heard and came to believe. In the garden, it was the serpent who changed the narrative surrounding God's prohibition against the forbidden fruit, twisting it until falsehood resembled truth. Time and again, we have been swayed into darkness by the words of others.

Of course, stories also illuminate the holy. Yet even when used for good, we must recognize stories hold immense power—to form, to persuade, to disciple.

Writers are curators of this power of words. As followers of Jesus, we are called to lay down that power and become servants. Therefore, our stories must also serve.

In laying down our power we come to storytelling from a place of humility, without agenda or prejudice. We simply tell, allowing the Word to use our words for His purposes. When we fashion our tales to make a particular point, we too are trying to control the narrative. But when we let the story unfurl on its own, we are trusting God will work through our open-handed offering. *Here is the story, Lord, as plain and true as a flawed human can possibly tell; make it Yours.*

Peacemaker and Benedictine nun Mary Lou Kownacki wrote, "There isn't anyone you couldn't love once you've heard their story." That is true, I believe, if those stories imbue *Imago Dei.*

Narrative power influences how we see others. We've all formed an opinion of someone—positive or negative—based on his or her story we've heard or read. However, we come to truly love others through their stories when their full dignity and worth as God's image bearers is displayed. The act of Christ-centric storytelling is revolutionary because it shows His creation as Jesus sees it:

- Bruised and beautiful.
- Struggling and shining.
- Frail and faithful.
- Overcome with ache and anger, hesitation and despair.
- Overflowing with hope and tenderness, generosity and song.

Our writing should turn the world upside down with Gospel clarity and, without proselytizing or pretense, lead to Emmanuel, God with us. He is the Story dwelling—seen and unseen—within the pages of every one of our stories.

And, by His grace, we are His storytellers.

Christa Parrish is a multi-award-winning author of five novels and the owner of Narratology, a social enterprise that empowers global artisans; all profits are used to buy the freedom of brick kiln bonded laborers in Lahore, Pakistan. Narratology.Gives

Celebrate Your Unique Style

Clarice James

*And whatever you do, whether in word or deed,
do it all in the name of the Lord Jesus, giving thanks
to God the Father through him.*

Colossians 3:17

God didn't throw away the mold when He made you. Why? Because there was no mold! He didn't look at you when you were born and announce, "Here she is! The new Karen Kingsbury!" Or "Whaddaya know, another Max Lucado!" Not even, "My, my, if it isn't Maya Angelou No. 2!"

You, dear writer, were not mass-produced.

And so, we need to ask ourselves: *Am I writing as the person the Lord intentionally created me to be? Is the "whatever" I offer done "in the name of the Lord Jesus, giving thanks to God the Father through him?"*

To determine if our "whatever" reflects our uniqueness (and gratefulness), we can ask ourselves these questions:

- Do I mimic the style of writers I admire?
- Do I discount my talent because I've never won an award?
- Am I building my platform on someone else's foundation?
- Do I doubt my worth because I'm not that deep and flunked the Mensa IQ challenge?

How about this soul-searching query: *Is my wishing and whining an insult to the omniscient God who purposely created me?* (Yikes!) Relax. Thankfully, God knows you and me and (still) loves us.

To get back on the writing path the Lord has specifically marked out for you, watch for glimmers of authenticity lighting your way.

What parts of the *real* you, the imperfect you, can you infuse naturally into your work? Perhaps one of your shortcomings shows up in your next protagonist. Maybe your merciful heart bleeds all over one of your blog posts. Or your abundant grace flows through an essay on forgiveness. Unplanned, your whimsical side pops up in a children's book, or your quirky sense of humor comes alive in your next novel.

Build on any faint sources of light you find.

When you write, use the original "voice" God endowed you with when He knit you together in your mother's womb. People don't want to hear a mediocre impersonation of another author while they're reading *your* words. Once you've rediscovered your voice, ask yourself which specific aspects of your writing need to be strengthened. Grammar? Structure? Scene-setting? Character development? Pace? Tension? Work on those skills through study and practice—not through imitation. Let whatever you absorb come out through the filter of *you*.

Receive God's writing assignments with thanksgiving as you celebrate your uniqueness. Pray for His anointing on your work and that He will multiply your gifts as you use them for His glory. Stop rubbernecking in literary circles, wishing you had someone else's skill or success. Remember, your shallow may be someone else's deep; your deep may be someone else's shallow. God can use us all!

Whatever you give, give as the best version of you, the person and writer who God created you to be.

Clarice G. James writes smart, fun, relatable contemporary women's fiction, weaving stories with colorful threads of faith, humor, romance, and mystery. When Clarice isn't writing, she's reading or encouraging fellow writers around New England. For more on Clarice go to ClariceJames.com

Saying Yes to the Unknown

Kim Findlay

*By an act of faith, Abraham said yes to God's call to travel
to an unknown place that would become his home.
When he left he had no idea where he was going.*
Hebrews 11:8 MSG

My love for maps started when I was little—finding towns and determining how to get from where I was to any place I wanted to be.

I fell in love with words about the same time I fell in love with maps. Words provided a way to navigate the intricacies of life. Even still, I often wondered if I had a story, something that was uniquely mine.

Then, everything shifted one spring morning in 2005. Fire roared through my home, destroying my journals, my pictures, our safety and, worst—it snatched the breath from my precious little girl.

I lost my words that day as I fell into my story. I didn't expect *that* story, the unknown and unwanted journey of grief.

Desperate for direction, I turned to the Author of all stories who knows the beginning, middle, and end. I scoured Scripture for people who endured similar sharp turns—Job, Joseph, Jeremiah, and Jesus—until one day I stumbled across these words:

"By an act of faith, Abraham said yes to God's call to travel to an unknown place that would become his home. When he left he had no idea where he was going" (Hebrews 11:8 MSG).

Was God calling me to say "yes" to this unknown journey? Abraham did. He was a man called to travel to a place he didn't know following a God he couldn't see. Was I willing to peer past my broken heart toward the promised end, fixing my gaze ahead as Abraham did?

Are you?

Abraham's courage to leave all he knew and embark on an unknown journey rested in God's faithfulness. And so, Abraham inspired me. I would say "yes" to this story God entrusted to me. Will you do the same with the story God has given to you?

With a quiet whisper, I chose to live like Abraham and embrace the invitation to have faith in the face of the unknown.

As God sustained me, I wrote. As He carried me, I cried into my journals. As He breathed life into my weary bones, I whispered words of praise for others to see.

All I needed was the courage to say "yes" to His call. I didn't know where I was going, but God gave me the ability to go and venture into His healing and His mercy. It was through saying "yes" that my words returned, and I found my story.

Do you feel like you've lost your words or your way? A diagnosis. A death. A detour away from what you knew that has disrupted your words. What might God be asking you to say "yes" to in the face of the unknown?

Kim Findlay is a writer, speaker, and ministry leader who loves to inspire hope and encourage people to grow in faith no matter their story. Her writing can be found at KimFindlay.com

God Has Heard Your Cry

Nancy Tupper Ling

*Hannah was speaking in her heart; only her lips moved,
and her voice was not heard ...*
1 Samuel 1:13 ESV

Is there anything worse than not being heard? As writers this can be an upsetting experience, especially if people aren't listening to our well-crafted words.

Has life ever cut so deeply that your heart welled up like Hannah's, and your lips were moving, yet you didn't have the voice to speak? Perhaps it seemed that even God wasn't listening to your pleas?

I know how Hannah felt. For five years Hannah's anguish over infertility was my own. But, today I have two daughters in college. I have to pinch myself when I say these words.

At first when we didn't conceive, my husband and I took time to travel, ballroom dance, and take classes. However, the longing soon became unbearable as I watched friends, family members, and virtual strangers having children with ease. Often, I cried out to God: *Aren't children a blessing, Lord? How much longer must we wait?"* I'm sure I appeared to be a drunken woman, as Hannah did to Eli the priest, because my lips were moving and my voice was not heard. Or was it?

Eventually, I realized God had been listening all along, but His timing was not my own.

On one memorable day, I lay down my will at last for God's will, while stretching prostrate on my bedroom floor. In return, I asked for one favor—that my words might go somewhere. *Even if I never get pregnant, Lord. Can just one person read my words?* God graciously answered. In time my first book, *Laughter in My*

Tent, was published, speaking to those who have experienced infertility.

Other poems and books followed. Amazingly, children did as well.

How does this relate to having the courage to write?

We all have experiences that take even more courage to survive than writing. Yes, getting words on the page is hard. The road to publication can be slow as molasses. Rejections sting!

Still, I'm reminded of a harder road—infertility, and how God walked with me. What painful time has God helped you through? If He was there then, He can surely bolster your spirit now as a writer.

Hannah's plea with God was the highest form of communion. She spoke with her heart. While the world assumed she was intoxicated, God heard her cries. When she bore her son Samuel, she gave him fully to the Lord. His very name means "I have asked for him from the Lord" (1 Samuel 1:20 ESV) or "God has heard."

If you are feeling unheard, remember that God knows the words you write. After all, isn't that the greatest reason we have to write with courage?

Nancy Tupper Ling is a children's author, poet, book seller, and librarian. She surrounds herself with books. Occasionally, she creates a few books and poems of her own, including her latest "For Every Little Thing" with co-author, June Cotner. NancyTupperLing.com

When Words Changed a Kingdom

Maureen Miller

*For if you remain silent at this time, relief and deliverance
for the Jews will arise from another place, but you and
your father's family will perish. And who knows but that you
have come to your royal position for such a time as this?*
Esther 4:14

Walking the writer's path can be a scary, even a threatening endeavor.

We live in precarious times. Our messages of hope in Christ are as important as ever but can cost us much. Do we waver in what we know we're to write? Is it difficult to send out our words knowing obedience to God's call may cost us friendships? Future opportunities? Others' approval?

Do our words even matter?

A young woman named Esther, her Hebrew name was Hadassah, could teach us much. Orphaned, she was raised by her cousin Mordecai, a Jewish man in exile. He instructed his adopted daughter to keep silent about her heritage when she was taken to the palace as a beauty queen contestant. We are not told the reason, but maybe Mordecai thought hardships could come to a Jew under King Xerxes' authority.

Obediently, Esther remained quiet.

When asked what supplies she wanted when it came her time to go before the king, Esther desired only what was recommended. She humbly acknowledged that another knew more than her about matters of outward beauty. Humility served

Esther well, and she was chosen—I like to think for the character of her heart. Remarkably, she became Queen of Susa.

When Mordecai discovered an evil plot to destroy the Jews, he urged Esther to go before her husband and plead for her people. Though she understood death was the penalty for approaching the king uninvited—apart, that is, from an extension of grace—she again chose to act upon the words of Mordecai, but not before three days of prayer and fasting. Esther knew doing so would birth wisdom and bolster courage.

She then committed to boldly go before the king, stating, "And if I perish, I perish" (Esther 4:16).

Esther displayed important qualities that we, as Christian writers in an antagonistic world, would do well to emulate.

- She was obedient.
- She was humble.
- She practiced spiritual disciplines to gain wisdom, glean courage.
- She was bold in proclaiming her message.

In short, Esther heeded her adopted daddy's words when Mordecai exhorted her, "And who knows but that you have come to your royal position for such a time as this?"

Her courageously spoken words turned the tide of impending destruction. Indeed, Esther's words changed the world.

Do you believe your words could be used to help change the world?

Directed by the King of Kings, our Abba Father, Savior, and Guide, our words have unlimited potential and supernatural power.

Yes, for such a time as this.

Maureen Miller lives on a hobby homestead in western North Carolina with her family and a plethora of animals. She desires to reach the world through words, share Jesus through stories and her blog about God's extraordinary character at PenningPansies.com

God's Not Through with You Yet

Kathleen O'Malley

Being confident of this, that he who began a good work in you
will carry it on to completion until the day of Christ Jesus.
Philippians 1:6

I was Ashamed. Heartbroken. Defeated.

Days earlier someone had told my teenage daughter that I wasted my writing talent and squandered my writing dreams. "Don't ever do that like your mother," she was cautioned.

Granted, my life didn't resemble that of a writer anymore. I worked in a call center and a second job as a store cashier to make ends meet. But I once led a writer's life.

I had been a successful journalist, an assistant editor at a literary magazine, and an editorial assistant at a small press. I had a graduate degree in writing and taught at two Boston colleges.

What happened to that person?

Divorce, and its accompanying financial devastation and upheaval had beaten me down.

Fear and self-doubt crippled me, and I stumbled off the writing path God paved for me. My writing community slipped away and attempts to find a solid writing group were unsuccessful. A box of short stories, my graduate thesis nominated for an award, sat in a box on a shelf for years, not one story submitted for publication.

I was in my fifties and couldn't see my way back to writing. *Well, I guess my writing life is over,* I told God one morning as I walked to work. As swiftly as the cars speeding past me on Kneeland Street in Boston, God refuted: "I'm not through with you yet."

Could it be that God had not given up on me even though I had given up on myself?

Paul assured Christians in Philippians 1:6 that being a Christian took time and commitment. There would be stumbling blocks, failures, and disappointments, but he urged them to not lose hope because what God started in each of them, He would finish.

Divorce, financial hardship, illness, the loss of a loved one, fear and self-doubt can derail our writing dreams for years, even decades. Thankfully, we are not in charge. God is. We can stand confident that what good work He begins, He will see to completion.

God is always true to His promises. I began publishing articles and writing fiction again. I joined American Christian Fiction Writers and found an amazing group of writers who hold me up when I feel like giving up.

I thought my writing life was over, but God had other plans. He has plans for you too.

God has called you to write. He is not through with you yet. When you are ready to give up, remember He always finishes what He starts, and He will see you through your writing journey.

Kathleen O'Malley is a former journalist who writes historical fiction and devotionals. She is a member of American Christian Fiction Writers and has a MFA in Creative Writing from Emerson College. She can be reached at KOMalleyTaylor@gmail.com

Fields of Hidden Treasure

Robin Farnsworth

Verily, verily, I say unto you, Except a corn of wheat
fall into the ground and die, it abideth alone:
but if it die, it bringeth forth much fruit.
John 12:24 KJV

I see J.G.'s neck first, brown as a pecan, barely covered by a crumpled straw hat, his white cotton shirt under a canvas seed sower.

"Let's go!" he says. Then he walks.

I put my hand to the small crank on the left of my seed bag and begin to follow. We are in a limitless field of brown dirt, the hazy South Carolina horizon stretching out before us like a life sentence. What did I get myself into now?

The field was for cattle, the seed for wheat. I had offered to work for my stay on this ranch. I was 20, landing like a comet from Manhattan to this small coastal island. It's 7 a.m. and I'm already sweating. J.G. was my grandfather's cousin, probably in his late 60's then, weathered to bone and sinew.

As he walks, he veers away from me, head down, arm cranking. Occasionally he calls, wiping dirt off a small object culled from the ground—a jagged piece of pottery, glass, or an arrowhead. The field owns a vibrant history scattered across the freshly plowed surface—Indians, Spaniards, and an 18th century family under small bleached crosses at the end of the field. *Treasure.*

Although it offered an intriguing rest, I was more focused on the shade-less task laid out before me, as the sun reared up like a fire breathing dragon.

I can't recall seeing that field turn green, although I'm sure it did. But what has sharpened in my memory over the years is how differently a young girl and an old man walked a field of plain dirt. I saw pain, tedium, and a lot of sweat. J.G. saw treasure.

Many years later, I stood before another barren landscape, but this one was my *entire life*. Where once grew the verdant blessing of God, now swallowed up the coffin of my firstborn child. It was hard ground, offering no promise, no hope.

Obedience can seem like death. Faith falters. The "high calling of God in Christ Jesus" is often heard where no one else is watching. *You can ditch that field and go lie in the shade. Who would blame you? Or you can walk. Jesus is there with your seed sower.*

"Follow me!" He says, and He goes before you, leaving hidden treasure along the way. And in time—His time—the buried seed bursts through the soil, "bringing forth fruit," God-fruit, like nothing you could ever dream of, or hope for.

A field of glory! But first, we walk, dear friend. So *let's go!*

Robin Farnsworth is an award-winning author and speaker. She and her husband live on Cape Cod and run Higher Ground Outreach, a ministry for the incarcerated and addicted. Learn more about how amazing Jesus is on her website: SpencersMom.com

Offering My 'Nothing' to God

Lori Stanley Roeleveld

*... as we look not to the things that are seen but to the things
that are unseen. For the things that are seen are transient,
but the things that are unseen are eternal.*
2 Corinthians 4:18 ESV

My blog had a very small readership.

At points, it could be discouraging, and I would wonder why I bothered to continue to write. It was especially hard at times when I so desperately wanted to make a difference.

One of those times arrived for me when, in 2010, Haiti experienced a devastating hurricane. I prayed asking God what I could do. Friends visited as part of disaster relief teams. Others donated financially. I felt I had nothing to give but God challenged me to write.

Write! That felt like nothing, I complained to God. *I have so few readers. What will writing a blog post accomplish?*

God quietly reminded me of the woman in 2 Kings 4. Elisha told her to go to her neighbors and gather all their empty jars. When she had gathered all of her "emptiness," God filled it with oil. God cautioned me that the only reason I didn't know what He could do with all my "nothing" is because I was still holding onto it and not offering it to Him.

And so, I wrote a blog post called "A Parable of Haiti, The American Church, and the Scandal of Responding to Those in Need." (Yes, the title was almost longer than the post.) I posted the article and waited. While I had more readers than usual, from what I could see, nothing really came of what I wrote. I imagined it was just an exercise in obedience.

Still, I kept writing.

To my surprise, in 2012, a friend told me she followed a New York Times best-selling author's blog, and that author was writing about me on her website! I didn't really believe it at first, but I went to her blog and, sure enough, there was an article where she referenced my 2010 blog post about Haiti.

While this famous author and her husband had been praying about donating to the work in Haiti and possibly ministering there, someone (I have no idea who) gave her a copy of my blog post from 2010. God used my article to convince this author to become involved in the work in Haiti and also to impact many of her countless readers.

I was grateful that someone with greater influence was joining in support of this need. But a totally unexpected byproduct was that overnight, my reader numbers increased dramatically, and my ministry began to multiply as never before.

God in His kindness provided me a glimpse of what for us writers is often unseen—the impact of our words on readers and His power to multiply our efforts.

We pray, write, and send words into the world—the rest is God's business. Much of what our words do, we won't know until we are home with Him in glory. Still, we must keep our eyes on what is unseen, so we do not weary of offering all of our "nothing" to Him.

Lori Stanley Roeleveld is a blogger, speaker, coach, and disturber of hobbits. Lori's authored four award-winning books, with a fifth releasing soon, and contributed to more. She speaks at women's events across the country. She speaks her mind at LoriRoeleveld.com

Finding Purpose in Our Pain

Melissa Pillone

I sought the Lord, and He answered me;
He delivered me from all my fears.

Psalm 34:4

Fear has to be one of the most intimidating and scariest words in the English vocabulary. Just thinking about fear brings visions of a racing heart, shaking knees, and sweating palms. There is nothing more frightening than facing our fears and pushing through them.

As a writer, the fear of how our writing will be received can keep the words we want to put onto paper locked away in our minds so that no one ever gets to read them. What a shame ! After all, God has blessed us with the creative gift of writing for a purpose such as sharing, inspiring, influencing, and educating.

As a teenager I made more than my share of bad decisions. Unrelenting temptation was waiting around ever corner. But the further I ran from my mistakes, the more entangled in my sins I became. As an adult I suffered from guilt and shame piled high, teetering and threatening to tumble down upon me, crushing me once and for all. Until I sought the Lord, confessed my sin, and received His forgiveness. Almost immediately, my pain was replaced by joy and I knew that God had a purpose for my life's story.

But when He called me to share it so others would know that they, too, are worthy of His love, grace and forgiveness, I argued. *No! I cannot talk about my past. I am too ashamed.* Fear of what others would think held me back.

God, though, continued urging and encouraging me, "I will be with you every step of the way." Clinging to that promise, I prayed for the right words to use, gathered courage to be vulnerable and wrote. Then I put my words out into the universe and prayed for God to use them. Oh, how He did!

I know that writing, telling, and sharing our personal stories can be scary.

Even after sharing my story many times, my heart still races and my knees still shake. However, I have witnessed something amazing takes place when we write and tell our stories for God's glory. He carries our message to those who need to hear it the most and He uses our message to transform lives and inspire change.

This reward far outweighs the fear felt at the beginning of the writing journey. Even better, with it comes the confidence to continue writing, knowing that God is right there with us. It may be *our* story we are telling, but when told well, there will be no doubt it was *coauthored with God*. Don't let fear keep you from that honor.

Melissa Pillone is a Christian writer and speaker who is passionate about sharing the good news of God's love, grace and forgiveness with others. You can find more about Melissa at MelissaPilloneSpeaks.com

Follow the Light

Cynthia Fantasia

You, LORD, are my lamp; the LORD turns my darkness into light.
2 Samuel 22:29

"I think you should write a book" he said.

I was at a conference a mere five days after my husband's memorial service. Two friends urged me to go with them, promising not to leave my side, and if I needed to exit one of them would take me home. Months earlier I had registered for this conference because a friend was one of the plenary speakers, and Bob was doing well at his new residence—a memory care center. His death was *not* on my radar.

And writing a book was the farthest thing on my mind that day.

But I told the man, who made that statement, that I would pray about it.

A few weeks later that man, who just happened to be a publisher, requested a book proposal, which sat on my computer for days. *This is not the right time. I have no idea what my future will be.* Those were days when I felt like I couldn't put a sentence together—much less a book.

One day, during my quiet time, I was reminded of my son's first year at private school, situated on a beautiful campus. In preparation for the first Back to School Night, parents received a letter advising us to wear comfortable shoes and bring a flashlight. *Interesting*, I thought at the time. That night we traversed rocky inclines, narrow stone steps, and little hills that would have caused many mishaps—except for the beam of our flashlights shining on each step just ahead of us.

Okay Lord, shine Your light on this proposal, I prayed as I tried to string words together that made sense.

A few weeks later I got a call that my proposal had been accepted. *Yikes, Lord, how can I do this?*

"Cynthia, I am your lamp, and I will turn your darkness into light—one step at a time." I heard the Lord "speak" deep into my heart. *Okay, Lord, shine your light on this writing journey.*

Finally, in July 2019 my first book *In the Lingering Light* was released to the world of Alzheimer's caregivers to offer courage and hope to weary hearts.

As I look back over those years of my own healing, intermingled with the monumental effort of writing a book, I think of the many days when I felt I couldn't write another word, and His light truly turned my darkness into light—and light-giving words.

Always remember that God never fails. His light always lingers over us—even in those slow and "dark" writing seasons!

———————————

Cynthia Fantasia served as Pastor of Women for 25 years at Grace Chapel, Lexington MA and speaks nationally and internationally. She is a contributing author in several books, and is author of "In the Lingering Light," NavPress, 2019. CynthiaFantasia.com

Let Your Voice Be Heard

Desiree Future

I can do all things through Christ who strengthens me.
Philippians 4:13

When God made you, He made you special. You may not have been born with a silver spoon in your mouth. You may not have grown up in the best part of town. Yet, God gave you something far more outstanding.

He gave you the gift of your voice.

Your voice is that powerful sound coming from deep within your soul. Expressing yourself by writing a poem, story, or a full-length novel is using your voice. This creativity can bring a smile to your face. This is *your* talent that God has bestowed upon you.

Fear often holds us back from using our voices.

After having cancer and going through grueling chemotherapy treatment, I was scared to begin writing again. I didn't know if I had the will to continue creating stories. The thought of letting anyone read my new compositions paralyzed me with fear. Though writing is my passion, I feared the unknown.

The thought of failing at something we really love is often the obstacle that stops us in our tracks.

So, how can we pick up our pens or put our fingers to the keyboard and start writing again? We ask God to give us strength.

Philippians 4:13 reads "I can do all things through Christ who strengthens me."

This verse got me through my illness and helped me carry on with my love of writing. It can help you, too.

Just as a child, learning to walk for the very first time, puts one foot in front of the other and moves forward, we take one step at a time.

Yes, we may fall more than once but we must keep getting up, just like a toddler doesn't give up.

We each have a story to tell that someone needs to hear. The power of our words can help heal the wounds of those who read our stories.

Oh, future writer and future author, let your voice be heard!

_____

Desiree Future is a native of New Jersey and enjoys traveling in her spare time. She writes Christian Fiction and Christian Romance. You will find her at DesireeFuture.com

Resolving to Tell Our Stories

Angela Nichole

Thou will keep him in perfect peace ...
Isaiah 26:3 KJV

The frayed leather of my office chair softly scratched my legs as I sat down to write my story.

My desk was littered with Bibles, books, highlighters, pens, and notebooks that I had accumulated throughout my life. Crumpled tissues rested in a pile just outside the small blue trash bin. The chaotic appearance of the desk matched that of my mind as I battled memories in my head.

We all have stories to tell.

It is rare to find someone making it into adulthood unscathed by this world. Writing the story can be cathartic, so I have been told; but it can also be scary and heart-wrenching to recall memories that leave a visceral mark. The vibrant thread of shame woven into this tapestry pushes the boundaries of intellect.

I was diagnosed with post-traumatic stress disorder (PTSD) when I was in my twenties.

A combination of diagnoses and medications followed for the next decade. Anxiety, depression, and bi-polar disorder were tossed around during my psychiatry sessions. I was a young mother trying to raise two young boys and be a sane wife; something that wasn't modeled for me. *How could I write about my most painful times and not get stuck in despair?* More importantly, *why would I want to write about them?*

Physical disability, self-worth issues, survivor's guilt, shame, and sexual trauma were in my rearview mirror but somedays it felt like I was driving straight into those storms. Living through them once was more than enough; the nightmares that plagued my mind were conflicts I thought I faced alone.

My inner fighter, the tenacity of my youth, refused to give up even as thoughts whispered in my head to end my life during one of my darkest hours. The TV blaring in the background that night did little to drown out the warfare in my head.

With tears streaming down my face, I called out to Jesus.

In that moment I realized the infallible faithfulness of Jesus despite my unfaithfulness to Him. He never stopped holding me even when I averted my eyes. My brokenness had led to laziness in all relationships, but most importantly in my relationship with Christ. I had forgotten Isaiah's words "Thou will keep him in perfect peace, whose mind is stayed on thee: because he trusteth in thee" (Isaiah 26:3 KJV).

I had forgotten how to put my trust in Him.

Remembering His grace and mercy, I have resolved to tell my story, for there is freedom in truth. I pray that you will also tell your story. And if you are bombarded by the memories of your past, I pray PTSD over you—Put your Trust in the Sovereign Deity.

Angela Nichole is a wife, mother, Christian blogger, and writer. She is a voracious reader, loves talking about Jesus, and lives by the words her dad instilled in her as a young child: adapt, achieve, and overcome. AngelaNicholeCity.com

When Pictures Become Words

Lauri Hawley

Then Christ will make his home in your hearts as you trust in him.
Your roots will grow down into God's love and keep you strong.
Ephesians 3:17 NLT

S napshots. All of my childhood memories are still-life snapshots.

- Picking up the heaviest rocks I could find from the bottom of the babbling brook running behind our house to build a dam that would stop the flowing water.
- Reading a book at the top of my favorite climbing tree, far out of my little brother's reach.
- Learning about Noah, David and Goliath, and Jonah in Sunday School.

Snapshots.

The only writing assignment I remember from my entire elementary school career involves just that—a snapshot. Our teacher handed out photographs and instructed us to simply write whatever came to mind. I have no idea what my photograph contained, but I do remember how exciting that assignment was!

Years later, after my children were themselves far beyond elementary school, I started writing again.

At first, I wrote encouraging newsletters to a group of local women. Then I began blogging, expanding the reach of the messages God gave me.

I wrote my first blog post in May of 2015. Without even realizing what was happening, I returned to that same school assignment each time I created a post. Whenever I saw something that aroused my curiosity or wonder, out flew my cell phone camera! Back at my computer, the image I had captured would begin as a mountain spring and become a flowing river of words.

Not just any words. The words almost always carried me back to spiritual roots that began developing in childhood: Those days in Sunday School reciting Bible verses. Bible stories that taught me to trust God's faithfulness in the face of life's trials and storms. Lessons that drove home the point that God *always* has a plan, even when I don't understand how any of it fits together.

God had a plan when He created me with a mind that thinks in pictures.

That school writing assignment was part of His plan, as was the newsletter, and now the blog. Each step of the process brought deeper growth and stronger faith.

My writing has ebbed and flowed through different seasons, but it has never completely dried up. My roots have continued to grow deeper and deeper into the love of the God who created me on purpose with a purpose. I trust Him to empower me in the days ahead to be a strong, worthy steward of the gift He has entrusted to me.

What about you, friend? How has God's handiwork come to life over the years through the talent He has given you? You, too, were created with a purpose! How will you step further into that purpose today?

———————————

Lauri Hawley is a wife, mother, grandmother, blogger, amateur photographer, and lover of getting dirt under her fingernails from digging in the flowerbed. She lives in Massachusetts with her husband, father, and two sons. You can visit her blog at LauriHawley.com

Why We Keep Writing

Christa Hutchins

*Let us not become weary in doing good, for at the proper time
we will reap a harvest if we do not give up.*
Galatians 6:9

R aise your hand if this has ever happened to you: God gave
you the most amazing opportunity to write a devotion. You
scoured every online concordance for insight into the key verse.
You poured your heart into sharing your hard story, agonizing
over every word and comma. It was perfect—your very best work.

Then a few days after submission, the dreaded rejection
letter arrived.

It's the final straw.

All writers have had this experience, or something similar. It
makes us wonder why we even try. *Why do we lay our souls bare
when no one is reading?* It feels like we've wasted not only our
time, but our story as well.

I'll tell you why. Because,

- God didn't tell us to stop. He had a reason for giving us
  this assignment. And if He's ever ready for us to stop,
  He'll tell us.
- God knew we would face struggles that would test our
  confidence in the message, and our faith in Him. And yet
  still, He called us.
- God has a plan for our stories, to redeem them and use
  them for His transforming glory. And He's trusting us to
  steward His plan.

So, we must "not become weary in doing good." We keep
writing. We keep sharing. We keep taking courageous steps

through every door He opens in front of us, even when we are tired and discouraged.

We wait for the proper time. God is going before us, preparing the way ... preparing the hearts who need our message. Be patient as He does His work.

He promises that we'll reap a harvest. Our harvest may look like an endless prairie field, or a small garden plot, or even a single brave seedling poking up through a cracked sidewalk. No matter what it looks like, the harvest is sure to come.

But only "if we do not give up." Only if we believe the victory that can come from sharing our stories is worth the struggle and pain that will come with the sharing.

I believe that is true for my story, and for yours. Let's promise each other that we'll trust, and wait, and reap with grace and humility. We'll keep writing even when no one is reading. We will not give up.

Christa Hutchins helps busy Christian communicators and leaders put structure and strategy around their big ideas through coaching and accountability. She lives in south Louisiana with her husband in their delightfully empty nest. Visit Christa at DoANewThing.com.

A Heart on Fire

Kirsten Panachyda

*These things I have spoken to you that in Me you may
have peace. In the world you have tribulation,
but take courage; I have overcome the world.*
John 16:33 NASB

The candle exudes the scent of a Parisian Cafe. An electric cup warmer holds my coffee at the perfect temperature. Satisfying my craving for tactile comfort, my Slinky moves under my fingers.

Despite the perfect set-up, the white screen and blinking cursor blast frost in my direction. I shiver from the stress and shame of it. I scold myself, *No distractions, and still no words. You claim to be a writer? Why are you even sitting here?*

And that's where shame makes its mistake. Because years ago, a wise teacher challenged me to find my "Why." On my desk sits a ragged piece of paper torn from a grocery list notepad that reads:

Because—
- God invites me to create with Him.
- Weary souls find courage in stories.
- Stories expand hearts and souls for more of God.
- God calls me to join His work of reaching hearts.
- Stories connect us to the "Great Story" of God and humanity.

"Take Courage!" Jesus tells us. In other translations, the verse says, "Take Heart!", "Be Brave!" or, "Be of Good Cheer!" Our oldest English translation, the 14th century Wycliffe Bible says "Trust ye!"

John uses the Greek word *tharseo* to convey the ideas of courage, cheer, bravery, heart, trust. This word is related to *therme*, which means heat, and *theros*, which means harvest-time, summer. *Tharseo* means to be bolstered from being warmed up, a radiant, warm confidence, or as the Greeks might have visualized it, a heart heated to readiness.

We can't manufacture the heat we need to tell the "Great Story" with candles, coffee, or toys. Even training, discipline, and sound methodology fail us. Blankets piled on a cold body only hold in the chill. We need the warmth from within.

Writers who want to join God in telling the "Great Story" need hearts heated to readiness. We need courage, heart, bravery, cheer, and trust. Jesus proclaims the source of the fire: "I have overcome the world!"

- Jesus—Savior, Friend, God with us has overcome.
- Jesus has *already, for all time* overcome.
- Jesus has overcome—won the war, settled every debt, emerged victorious.

Dear writer, this very Jesus invites us to create with Him. Can you feel the glow in your soul? Do you know your "Why?" Does your work radiate from your joy in the "Great Story?"

Tharseo is a way to be, a manner of living, a faith adventure. When we write or speak, may our tools and preparation serve our calling. May troubles of distraction, deadlines, or imposter syndrome melt in our confidence.

May we carry the promise to our hearts, heating them into the readiness of courage.

Kirsten Panachyda writes to infuse courage into the soul-weary, especially parents of kids who have mental illness. She also writes historical fiction. She will return from daydreaming about ancient Britain for a cup of coffee or to connect at KirstenP.com

Let God Be Your Editor

Tamson Jensen

He will not be afraid of bad news.
His heart is strong because he trusts in the Lord.
Psalm 112:7 NLV

W hen my daughter was too young to read, she would look at picture books, make up her own stories, and "read" them to us.

This amused her Papa because she would dramatically render her version of the story. He would then read the book verbatim, after which she would confidently declare, "Thanks, Papa, but I like *my* story better."

This scenario feels familiar to me in my "grown-up" world. I ask God about His will for my life—thrilled to be part of His great story—but I don't always like His answer. It's not the story *I* want to tell.

I'd rather be God's editor, giving Him notes like, "This stuff about forgiveness, sacrifice, loving your enemies ... not very marketable ideas."

Like my daughter, I find myself saying, "Thanks, God, but I like *my* story better."

And so, I had this vision of how my life would go, but (surprise!) things didn't fall neatly into place. I didn't want to tell a story that included a failed marriage, or the grief of infertility, or the pain of parenting an adopted child haunted by trauma.

I wanted to tell a story full of joy, with a predictable Hallmark ending!

But what's a good story without mystery and conflict? How could I truly know joy without sorrow? How could I know the depth of God's grace without my human failings?

When I was young and anticipating my future, I just wanted to survive and skip to the ending to avoid the uncomfortable mystery in the middle.

I found myself avoiding writing to avoid the reality of life.

When my marriage was falling apart, I mysteriously stopped journaling for a season. Eventually, my internal struggle became unbearable, and these were the first words that finally poured out onto the page: "I didn't want to write about this because that means it's real."

It takes courage to be real, to own our stories, even (and especially) when life unfolds in unwanted or unpredictable ways.

But I've learned that the mystery and conflict is where grace happens, where we learn to love, where we learn to let go and trust.

I love what Richard Rohr says, "The most courageous thing we will ever do is to bear humbly the mystery of our own reality. That is everybody's greatest cross."

These days, instead of "making up" the clean, tidy story I wanted to tell, I embrace the messy, beautiful story I have lived— one that is still unfolding.

Turns out, God's version of my story is rich and full of wonder, challenging and unpredictable, and *far* better than the story I would have written for myself.

I'm grateful He disregarded my edits.

Tamson Jensen is a chatty, irreverent Southerner who loves good stories, coffee, baked goods, reading, writing, taking pictures, singing, shopping, and hanging out with her husband of 20 years, their five kids and five grandkids. You can read more of her ramblings at TamsonJensen.com

Writing as an Act of Worship

Meadow Rue Merrill

Therefore I urge you, brethren, by the mercies of God,
to present your bodies a living and holy sacrifice,
acceptable to God, which is your spiritual service of worship.
Romans 12:1 NASB

Did you know the Hebraic word for "worship" comes from a word meaning "to serve" or "to work?"

This was explained to me by a rabbi when I was a student, studying for a semester at a Christian college with stone archways and fortress-like walls overlooking the Hinnom Valley in Jerusalem.

Growing up in church, I'd always thought of worship as something that involved singing—the louder the better.

But this rabbi explained that in Jewish culture, worship includes everyday activities such as studying, working with your hands, or helping a neighbor. I understood this to mean that worship encompasses any activity that involves the right use of our minds or bodies in service to God.

Changing dirty diapers? Check! Stacking wood for a sick neighbor? Check! Crawling out of bed at 4:30 a.m. to write the next chapter of your novel? Check! By the Jewish definition, each of these actions qualifies as worship when done in a way that pleases our Creator.

In nearly three decades of earning a living as a writer, I freely confess that for me the hardest part of writing—harder than finding an agent or a landing a mega book contract—is maintaining the right motivation.

How easy it is, particularly when perusing social media, to compare my work to the work of other writers, pining for celebrity success. Not that I want to actually *be* a celebrity. But oh, to see my hard work recognized at the top of a best-seller list!

For many writers, this type of thinking leads in only one direction: disappointment.

But when I begin my day by offering my work to God, *Here I am Lord. Use my writing today in any way that You wish. Fill my mind with Your thoughts and Your words so that they may bring honor and glory to You ...* my words are transformed into worship.

In Romans 12:1, the apostle Paul paints a picture of what true worship looks like: laying my work on God's altar and offering it to Him. When I do this, my work is no longer mine, but God's, and I find myself free to truly write. Free from self-judgment. Free from selfish ambition. Free from pride.

Scripture calls us to offer to God not only our bodies, but the *work* of our bodies—the early mornings and late nights stringing words and images and stories together on a page. Then, by God's mercy, our words become more than words. They become living and holy, a sacrifice acceptable to God—our spiritual service of worship.

Meadow Rue Merrill, author of "Redeeming Ruth" and of the Lantern Hill Farm children's picture book series, writes from a little house in the big woods of Midcoast Maine. Connect at MeadowRue.com where you can find her blog, Faith Notes.

The Key that Opens Every Door

Melanie Shull

I have set the LORD always before me;
because he is at my right hand, I shall not be shaken.
Psalm 16:8 ESV

I love to go for walks. The warmth of the sunshine on my face, the fresh air in my lungs, and my feet pulsating to a moderate tempo awakens my senses and refreshes my soul.

Faith-walking also heightens our spiritual senses, especially our sight. When our eyes are fixed on Jesus, our faith cannot be shaken. But, when our focus shifts downward to our inabilities, like Peter walking on the water, we become weak, lose our balance, stumble, and fall.

So, how do we keep our focus on Jesus?

Just like our physical muscles need to be stretched every day, so do our faith muscles. As our faith strengthens, our spirit syncs into rhythm with our Savior. A strong faith provides us the courage we need to completely trust in Jesus Christ.

Without faith, there is no courage. Without courage, there is no obedience. And obedience? It's the evidence of our faith.

When God called me to publish a magazine, I was ecstatic, afraid, and ill-equipped. I wasn't even a writer. Nonetheless, after years of walking with the Lord and experiencing His faithfulness, I've learned that blind faith has amazing benefits, and at times, ignorance can be bliss. God never assigns His children a task without providing the tools to complete the work. Faith is key, but it takes courage and strength to turn that key.

If my faith muscles had been weak, I would not have mustered the courage to open the door to my first writing assignment. If my eyes had wandered, I would have missed out on the grace-full adventure of learning and practicing the art of writing.

Encouraging followers of Christ to examine their real-life stories through the lens of faith, and helping them craft their stories to encourage others, has brought me more joy than "Christmas in a cup." (A peppermint chocolate chip milkshake—Heaven!)

Having the courage to publish *Living Real Magazine* was only the beginning. With every writing assignment, my faith and courage have grown stronger, and saying "Yes" to my assignments has become easier.

How about you? How strong is your faith? How are you stretching your faith muscles to build up the courage to write for God's glory?

Remember, eyes up. Walk with Jesus. Obey His Word. Pray continuously. If you set the Lord before you, you will not be shaken. Have courage, sweet friend, and until your faith is made sight, go write. Then, celebrate with a milkshake.

———————————

Founder and Chief Editor for Living Real Magazine, author Melanie Shull loves hosting Jesus-centered conversations surrounded by coffee and chocolate. Her Bible study/memoir, "Unlocked Hearts, Unleashed Joy: Forgiveness Is the Key" is available on Amazon. LivingRealMag.com

Who Will Inherit
Your Words?

Julie Kieras

*We will not hide them from their children, shewing to
the generation to come the praises of the Lord, and his strength,
and his wonderful works that he hath done.*
Psalm 78:4 KJV

"Write your testimony. In Spanish."
My eyes grew large at this challenge from our Uruguayan mission team leader. Not only had I never written my testimony down before, but now I had to write it in a language I'd only been studying for a few years. It felt like being asked to write an epic novel blind-folded and with my left hand. I feared I would sound choppy or use the wrong phrase or verb tense. What if I said "pregnant" instead of "embarrassed" (a common error for beginning Spanish speakers!)

I felt a poverty of words before people who trilled Spanish easily from their lips. How could I share the treasure of the Gospel story in a language not my own?

Isn't this how writing often feels, even in our native tongue?

When I sit to write, I fumble with the very words I love so much. The words that soar within my heart fall foreign onto the page. They look black and white compared to the technicolor of my imagination. So, I set the pen down. I close the computer. I tell myself to give my time to something more obviously profitable.

On my mission trip to Uruguay, my work became to prayerfully find the courage to speak in a language not my own. Much the same, we as writers must find courage to write—even when it feels foreign to us. There's someone—perhaps even another writer—waiting to hear how God has worked mightily.

Bridging generations with words has always been God's specialty. Through spoken prophecy, songs passed down from tribe to tribe, or written words via letter and scribe, God has always told people to share the story of His goodness.

The command to the people of Israel was *Don't forget, don't hide your testimony.* Our experiences with God are not for hiding. We don't praise God alone in the dark. No, we write about hardship, pain, growth, and gain. We have a wealth here that only grows by sharing. So, we couch these treasured moments of intimacy in words, creating an inheritance to pass along. God's present provision becomes a legacy.

Every word you write is *your testimony of courage and hope* in the Lord. Whether we write novels, poetry, articles, devotionals, or Bible studies, each time we set down these wild and wonderful words, we bear testimony: *God is always working!*

Writing is a generational work filled with hope but born of courage. God opens our lips to speak and our pens to write. In this inheritance of words, God's strength works miracles often unseen.

Writing is our song, our shout, our hand reaching out in the dark, touching generations.

Julie Kieras is a wife and mom of two boys. On her blog, Happy Strong Home, she shares encouragement and resources for parents who desire to grow a happy, strong family that loves God. Read more at HappyStrongHome.com

Learning to Embrace the Ordinary

Jennifer Drummond

Teach us to number our days, that we may gain a heart of wisdom.
Psalm 90:12

"Did you know," the well-dressed woman began, "that the words ordinary and ordinal have the same root?" Huh, I thought to myself, furiously scribbling notes, I did not know that.

"They are Latin, meaning row, rank, or regular arrangement. Both have to do with counting or arranging things of importance."

Was it just possible that ordinary time—the long stretch between the season of Pentecost (mid-June) and Advent (the weeks before Christmas)—might be so called because those are important days and ought to be, well, ordered accordingly? This thought wiggled its way into my brain as I fell asleep to the sounds of cicadas and the summertime breeze. It percolated during the full days of that conference.

But as I returned home to my life, with husband, children, and dog all happy but each needing something, I quickly forgot about ordinals in the crush of ordinary.

A few months later, I read Psalm 90:12, "Teach us to count our days," and that forgotten thought was back. Huh. I glanced out the window at the golden cascade of morning light, the turning leaves pulling at something poignant within me. Counting and ordering were related, and it had to do with what was important. I closed my journal and pondered until I heard footsteps on the stairs, and that thought slipped once again out of consciousness in the barrage of breakfast and backpacks.

Sitting alone with my husband in the glow of the Christmas tree lights, while quiet and comfortable, the thought surfaced again. *Why had Advent this particular year been meaningful?* I wondered. Was it something to do with counting the weeks until Jesus' arrival—those ordinal first, second, third, and fourth Sundays? Was it to do with ordering our days around the waiting together in darkness? I wasn't entirely sure and decided that pausing my writing and work, to just be, was enough for now.

I glanced out my window hoping to see green buds, but only bare sticks on the hydrangea were visible. The piece I was writing frustrated me too. I contemplated closing my computer for good, when ordinal time surfaced again. "Teach us to number our days." Somehow, I knew that it was important to not give up, but to embrace this day and time for the work God had given me. I stopped only when my son gave me a hug, bringing me back to the present.

What season and stage of life are you in right now? When does it take courage to pick up your pen and write? When does it take courage to put down your pen and engage in ordinary life?

Jennifer Drummond orders her days in Hamilton, Massachusetts with her family. As a spiritual director, she contemplates the seasons through photography, offers online retreats, blogs somewhat regularly, and reads voraciously by the fireplace. Find her at JADrummond.com

Tell What He Has Done!

Sheryl Holmes

"… let me tell you what he has done for me."
Psalm 66:16

One day I asked my grandson the proverbial question: "Which came first, the chicken or the egg?" We have nine faithful hens that feed us well and he loves to collect the eggs. But at my question, a kind of paralyzed look came over his face and he could not answer confidently.

For even seasoned Christians, next to the chicken and egg question, stands this one: What is God's will for me? Many who walk with Jesus pause with a kind of paralyzed look and cannot answer the question confidently. The apostle Paul tells us quite clearly what the will of God is for all of us: rejoice, pray, and give thanks in all situations (1 Thessalonians 5:16-18).

This is an encouragement for writers because these actions—rejoice, pray, and give thanks—demand a voice.

The Psalms are full of examples of voice, and with it, many invitations: "Come and hear, all you who fear God; let me tell you what he has done for me" (Psalm 66:16). How can we tell what God has done unless we use our voices?

As co-laboring writers with me, I ask you, *Have you found your voice and will you raise it?*

All the power is in the story; "let me tell you what he has done for me." Each of us has a uniquely spun story to tell and yet, each story is the same—God has done it.

Our stories may be like that of a toddler who takes his first step. He is good for three, maybe four, steps in a row and then, you know what happens, he falls. He may have a scrape, a bump, and cry. But always, a parent is ready nearby to pick up the child and set him right again.

Our stories are *I fall, I am set right by my Father, and I walk again*. Through loss, illness, and hardship—this is my story—"let me tell you what he has done for me."

After a still born baby, God gave me peace; through surviving cancer twice, God sustained me; after my son died of an unexpected drug overdose, God gave me hope. Yes, I am a Christian. Yes, I am real.

When Christians are transparently real, our experiences resonate with those who lack a relationship with Jesus.

My will in Christ Jesus as a Christian writer is to use my written voice to point to Jesus and embrace the power of story to touch the hearts of all who need to hear how good our Lord is.

Join me! Use your voice and tell others what God has done for you!

———————

Sheryl Holmes, used by God to encourage others with the written word. An author and speaker from Belchertown MA, doing her best to point to Jesus, the everlasting lover of our souls. InTheBattle.org

I Read It In a Book

Karen Porter

*Let my teaching fall on you like rain; let my speech
settle like dew. Let my words fall like rain on tender grass,
like gentle showers on young plants.*
Deuteronomy 32:2 NLT

Do words have the power to change a life?
"[God] unveils the myth of flawlessness and calls Christians to come out of hiding and stop pretending."

"Holiness is not a bid to be noticed or loved or accepted by God. Holiness, rather, is acting out and acting upon the truth that God has noticed, loved, and accepted us long before we did anything to warrant that."

"Bold prayers honor God and God honors bold prayers. If it's not impossible to you, it is insulting to God."

"If you aren't hungry for God, you are too full of yourself."

Where did I find such amazing words of wisdom? I read them in a book.

The first quote about pretending came from *Messy Spirituality* by Michael Yaconelli. I believed if I followed the rules, I could be a good Christian. But this book shined a light, revealing the pretense hidden in my heart and gave me the courage to develop a deep relationship with my Savior.

I read the second quote in the book, *Your God is Too Safe* by Mark Buchanan. I wallowed in a low spiritual valley until those sentences changed my outlook. Through Buchanan's words, I discovered how much God cherishes me. He adores me not because of what I accomplished, but He loves me because He loves me.

The third quote about bold prayers is highlighted on a worn page in the book *Circle Maker* by Mark Batterson, because I doubted I should bother God with my dreams and desires. But He put those ambitions in my heart, and when I pray about anything, God listens.

Mark Batterson also shocked me with the words of the fourth quote about being full of myself in his book *All In*. I was traveling in a foreign country for my job, and I was frustrated because some parts of the trip didn't turn out the way I'd expected. His words changed my perspective. My job was not me, and my climb up the corporate ladder didn't draw me closer to God.

When God called me to write, I wanted to write life-changing words. To influence one person, changing their life with words from my pen—words which I know came from above.

- Be courageous to write because some young mom needs to read your words so she can make it through the day of toddlers and diapers.
- Write the words because some lonely traveling executive may have tucked your book into her luggage, hoping for words of encouragement.
- Say it plain and powerfully because some Christian may need to break out of a stronghold and live a life of trusting God. In the dark night of someone's grief, your words may give light.

So, write!

Karen Porter is an international retreat and seminar speaker and a successful businesswoman. She is the author of eight books. Karen coaches communicators in writing and speaking and has coached thousands of speakers across the globe. Reach her at KarenPorter.com

Flourishing with Words

Stephanie Goddard

*But if we walk in the light, as he is in the light,
we have fellowship with one another, and the blood of Jesus,
his Son, purifies us from every sin.*
1 John 1:7

Weeds

A tiny sprout emerges, appears as nothing at first
Then brings a certain beauty—green against brown earth

It thrills winter-tired eyes; No harm, so let it be
It stretches, spreads and grows, but not only what you see

Green grows above the earth, outside, a harmless shoot
But underneath the surface hides the deep, insidious root

Anchored verily, tight to earth, a thick and viny web
Relentless, tenacious, healthy, strong, invades as now it spreads

Thorns and thistles thrive, abound; We toil to destroy them now
We pull, we dig, we struggle and work by the sweat of our brow.

On our small farm, as spring turns to summer and our fields burst with growth, other plants appear, ones we didn't sow. They seem harmless enough at first. But left to the natural progression, they will stifle the garden's beauty, choking the loveliness until the only thing visible is the unwanted plants and a harvest of weeds.

My definition of a weed is something that grows where you don't want it.

As writers, we may encounter all sorts of weeds. They can be weeds of unhealthy comparison, worry, or self-doubt.

Our heavenly Father doesn't want these negative thoughts for us. If allowed to germinate, these will eventually overwhelm the work the Creator intended. But like a good farmer, our loving Master provides the tools we need to face these challenges.

On our farm, if we want to deal with a significant weed problem, we cover the plot with a large, black tarp. Eventually, the weeds are starved for light, and shrivel and die.

Doubts and sin, on the other hand, need darkness to thrive. So how do we combat them? Smother them with light.

Light, by its very nature, dispels darkness. 1 John 1: 5-7 says "God is light and in Him is no darkness at all … But if we walk in the light, as He is in the light, we have fellowship with one another and the blood of Jesus his Son, purifies us from all sin."

How do we walk in the light? How do we allow the light of Jesus to conquer the weeds of doubt?

Pray. Listen to His voice. Meditate on His Word. Spend time in His presence. Have fellowship with one another in open, accountable relationships. Let His light shine into every part of you. Bring even the seemingly harmless negative thoughts into His light. Lay your doubts and fears before him and, in His light, they will shrivel.

Remember what He has called you to. Your garden will flourish with the words He's given you to write.

Stephanie Goddard is a wife, mom, Grammie, farmer, and Christian author from New Hampshire. She writes contemporary women's fiction and romance. Her desire is to show through story the mighty, redemptive, and healing power of the cross of Christ.

Walking Hand-in-Hand With God

Tammy Gerhard

See, I am doing a new thing! ...
Isaiah 43:19

Three in the morning found me flat on my face on the floor at the end of my bed.

As I lay there, I heard as if in a dream: "I am stripping away everything comfortable for you. From now on you will be over your head. Take My hand and do only what I tell you. When I want you to write, you'll put your fingers to the keyboard and words will flow. If it doesn't happen that day, don't think about it. When I want you to speak, I'll open the door for you to do it and give you the words. If it doesn't happen that day, don't worry about it. From now on you are to go low, take My hand, and do only what I show you."

In a half-dream state, I climbed back into bed and went to sleep.

When I finally woke up, I knew what I had heard meant I was leaving my position as a school counselor—the job I had loved for over 13 years, and where I assumed I would stay until retirement. It also meant starting the one thing I'd never considered—writing.

However, the Lord in His goodness had prepared a path of support for me in advance. In an earlier season of life, I had met an author who'd spoken these words to me: "You are going to write one day."

For the first time in my life, I began to believe it might happen. I prayed, called my author friend, and shared what happened.

She quickly included me in a writers' event she was hosting, arranging for me to meet with a nationally recognized author for counsel and direction.

God uses others to encourage us on our journey.

The first time I wrote a blog post I almost had an anxiety attack. I was truly in over my head in the most vulnerable of ways. There is something so raw about revealing a part of yourself to the public, inviting others to read and comment. The response however was filled with support, including comments asking why I'd not done this sooner.

While these encouragements are comforting to read, they are not why I write. As God promised, there are days I wake with words on my mind. I take out my laptop and they flow. I hit publish and trust He will use them.

But on days when the writing doesn't come, I do other things. I obey and trust the outcome to Him.

God has been faithful to His words shared early that morning while my head was on the cold wooden floor.

That moment opened the door to a new season of life for me, one where I walk hand-in-hand with Him and am given the courage to write. God can do the same for you.

Tammy Gerhard is a writer, speaker, counselor, mentor, and friend. She delights in sharing stories over hot lattes and cookies at the local coffee shop she co-owns in the center of her town.

Trusting When God Calls You

Myra Ingargiola

Forget the former things; do not dwell on the past.
See I am doing a new thing! ...
Isaiah 43:18-19

A s I walked toward the door into the writer's conference a great weight hindered me.

Three times I'd allowed the burden to stop me.

Three times I'd gone back and forth from my car to the front door in an attempt to trust God and step across that threshold. I tried to ignore the burdensome sensation by telling myself my bags were simply heavy. But no, this was not just the physical weight of luggage.

I'd been so sure God was leading me here, to this new thing. I'd been so excited. Now, though, all my thoughts shifted to fear and inadequacy, as an imagined voice spoke over me. *You don't have what it takes to be a writer or a speaker*, it whispered.

Like stones in my pockets, those negative words weighed me down. And, believe me, an excessive number of stones piled up. They formed the burden, and a sense of oppression that became so overwhelming, defeat seemed more appealing.

I carried these familiar stones into every Holy Spirit-led opportunity to share my story as a speaker or writer. They prevented me from what God had called me to be—a voice for Him.

Standing at the conference center door, I knew I must surrender to my wonderful Savior and take that fearful step forward into the unknown, into the new.

The movie *The Last Crusade* with Indiana Jones came to mind. At the end, Jones makes the choice to take a step across the threshold into the uncertain. He whispers, *Only a penitent man shall pass*, trusting that God would grant Him safe passage into that which was obscure.

Like Jones, I now stood at the threshold. Taking a deep breath, I submitted myself before God and whispered, *Not my will, but yours.*

A quiet, gentle whisper "Forget the former things; do not dwell on the past. See, I am doing a new thing!" replaced the unyielding, discouraging words.

The negative words I'd been clutching onto held no purpose other than weighing me down in untruths. But the Holy Spirit radically loosened their power over me, resurrecting a new freedom.

I turned my pockets inside out and, one by one, discarded every stone that had invalidated me, and made me ineffective.

I was free to bask in the truth that God placed me here. He brought me into this "new thing" for His glory. I only had to trust His timing, His purpose, and His affirmation.

Are you willing to trust God when He calls you to His higher purpose? I encourage you to empty your pockets of all that is weighing you down and step out in faith!

Myra Ingargiola's deepest passion is sharing her life stories by weaving a tapestry of God's love, grace, and mercy. As a writer and speaker she is committed to leading others toward a deeper faith-filled life.

Persistent in Prayer

Cindy Saab

*Devote yourself to prayer, keeping alert in it with an attitude
of thanksgiving; praying at the same time for us as well,
that God will open up to us a door for the word, so that we
may speak forth the mystery of Christ, for which I have
also been imprisoned; that I may make it clear in the way
I ought to speak. Conduct yourselves with wisdom toward
outsiders, making the most of the opportunity. Let your
speech always be with grace, as though seasoned with salt,
so that you will know how you should respond to each person.*

Colossians 4:2-6 NASB1995

To be effective Christian communicators we must be devoted to prayer.

The Greek word for "devote" means "to be courageously persistent." Our prayers for ourselves and for the recipients of our written and spoken words are to be bold and persistent.

Using the Colossians passage above, I have developed guidelines for "Courageously Persistent Prayer" for Christian communicators:

- Prayer: Surrender and devote your writing and speaking ministry to the Lord. Join others in constant prayer (Acts 1:14, Romans 12:12), "pray at all times ... and stay alert with all perseverance and intercession for all the saints" (Ephesians 6:18 CSB).
- Persistent: Be persistent even when discouragement sets in and all you see are the insurmountable obstacles. Be persistent daily in shifting your focus on the Lord and your calling.

- Open Door: Pray for God to open a door for your message, to share the Gospel (Colossians 4:3), and "a great door for effective work" (1 Corinthians 16:9).
- Clarity: Ask to write with clarity, grace, and purpose to the glory of His Name (Colossians 4:6).
- Wisdom: Seek godly wisdom in how you write, speak, and act—to be a good steward of your time and wise in the selection of projects; to get the rest and healthy nutrition your human body craves.

Dear Heavenly Father, we thank you, Lord, that we are children of God called to share a specific message. We praise You for Your anointed calling to communicate and write powerful transforming messages. We pray for a tenacity to continue and "march on" when life is hard and for the Holy Spirit to infuse us with Your strength when we are exhausted physically, emotionally, and spiritually. We ask that You give us courage and a holy boldness to say "yes" to Your assignment(s) that You appointed to us before the beginning of time. May every word we speak and word we write bring "the glory of Your Name"! Amen.

Cindy Saab is an author, speaker, teacher, and coach. She loves networking and cultivating relationships to encourage and equip others traveling through unexpected seasons/storms. An award-winning Bible study author, she is the mother of two adult children and resides in New England. CindySaab.com

Your Distinguishing Mark

Jane Rubietta

*I, Paul, write this greeting in my own hand, which is
the distinguishing mark in all my letters. This is how I write.*
2 Thessalonians 3:17

Rows and rows of colorful, best-selling books wrapped around
me in this amazing bookstore. Why would *I* imagine myself
a writer?

One glance at the books facing out from their perches, their
high visibility a sure sign of popularity, sent my head down. *I
could never write like those authors.*

But I remembered how words saved me, as a pastor's wife in
a rural area, with new babies and no car, and long-lasting post-
partum depression. My searching for answers, for help, for hope.
Words soon filled journals, and the lifeline of creativity and connecting with God boosted me from those rural deeps.

During the long, jagged process of healing, I opened conversations with women in our teeny church: about anger, depression,
and boundaries. Their eyes brightened in recognition, and sometimes filled with tears. They asked, "Why isn't anyone writing
about this?"

That's when I heard the very clear call from God. "You can
write this." Even now, I feel a turning in my chest, as though a
key fits the exact lock holding all those words in silence.

Still, the question remained: *what do I have to say that someone else couldn't say, with more eloquence or cleverness?* Sadly, that
doubt still hovers, many years and words and articles and books
since that countryside calling.

Paul's closing words to the Thessalonians seem, at a glance, unremarkable. "I, Paul, write this greeting in my own hand, which is the distinguishing mark in all my letters. This is how I write."

As a writer, again and again I read this verse, a litany:

- This is how I write.
- This is my own hand.
- My distinguishing mark.

Not someone else's hand. Not another's voice. *My* hand, *my* tone, *my* voice. *my* story.

Comparison destroys courage and creativity. Look instead at your own calling and gifts. No one else can write the words you and I write. No one else has the exact journey to give our words wisdom and credibility. No one else can take your place. Your unique hand, tone, voice need to be released. Perhaps they are the very lifeline a reader needs—just one reader—to be lifted out the deeps.

Paul likely never expected that two thousand years later, we'd be reading his words. He wrote, not for glory, but for salvation to be released in the world.

Next time you visit an amazing bookstore, I hope you will remember this. Whether your book ever props face-out on a shelf, or your face graces a magazine cover; whether your words garner a living wage, or the occasional like on a blog, we are not writing to make a living.

We are writing to live. And to help others live.

Jane Rubietta writes in her own hand in the Midwest. A writing and speaking coach, she cofounded Life Launch me, helping people live their dreams. She speaks internationally, has written hundreds of articles and 21 books. Reach her at JaneRubietta.com

Susan E. Moody

God Designed Us Well for the Task

Susan E. Moody

*I praise you because I am fearfully and wonderfully made;
your works are wonderful, I know that full well.*
Psalm 139:14

As a kid, I felt like a misfit.

I was the second of four children. Bobbi was "The Oldest." Becky was "The Youngest." Brian was "The Only Boy." Sometimes I felt like I had no special place in the family. Our names didn't help—my siblings were named Bobbi-Jo, Brian Joseph, and Becky Jane … and I am Susan Elizabeth. Then there's my hair—everyone in the family had dark straight hair, but I was a curly blonde.

I had a great childhood and a loving family, but reality and perception are not always the same thing. I felt like a misfit.

Sometimes I feel like that with my writing as well. I look at other writers and what they produce. I see their success and the fans who love their work. I feel like I don't fit in as a writer.

Even worse, I feel afraid to even try.

I am good at writing poetry—but not the broodingly romantic type that I long to produce. My talent is with the Dr. Seuss kind. Rewriting song lyrics or jotting a birthday poem is simple—a party trick meant for special occasions.

But I always doubted that God could use it for Kingdom purposes.

Fifteen years ago, I wrote a seminar focused on Psalm 139 to teach others to base their self-worth on being made in God's image. I often emphasize the lessons in my seminars with children's books, but I could not find a book with just the right message for my Psalm 139 seminar. Then, on the way to church one Sunday morning, the first line of a poem popped into my head. By the following Wednesday the poem was complete.

As I shared my words with others, it quickly became clear that my talent for poetry had been used by God to craft a poem that would speak God's truth to the hearts of children and adults. Four years later I published it as a children's book and have sold almost 2000 copies.

Writing takes courage.

Whether staring at a blank page or handing our work over to others for feedback, the process can cause us to question ourselves. We doubt whether we have the right talents—whether God designed us well for the task.

But Psalm 139, especially verse 14, puts our mind to rest on that point. Each of us was purposefully designed by God. We were carefully planned out and put together. All of God's works are wonderful, and since we are one of those works, we can know that we are "fearfully and wonderfully made."

Will you embrace that truth today? That knowledge gives us courage to bravely write for God's glory.

Rev. Susan E. Moody loves to help others learn God's truth as an ordained CCCC minister, with a BA from Gordon College, an MA from Geneva College, and a MDiv from Gordon-Conwell Theological Seminary. She can also hang a spoon on her nose.

The Courage to Share

Debbie Lowe

I lift up my eyes to the hills. From where does my help come?
Psalm 121:1 ESV

Do I share this or not?

Sharing personal stuff, problems, and challenges is hard. What will others think of me? Of my family? Is it fair to share about my experience of a family problem?

Our adopted daughter was a special needs child. Not the kind of need that's immediately apparent, but a need that had been camouflaged for years.

Fearing that others, especially family and friends, would discover the depth of her issues, my husband and I struggled to hide them—at our own expense. We set strict boundaries with consequences hoping our daughter would make safe, healthy choices. From the outside it appeared we were treating her unfairly; we endured undeserved and sometimes harsh judgment from others.

No matter how hard we tried, we failed.

Then we experienced a couple instances of stealing from family members, followed by an email (written on a family member's computer) alleging abuse.

By her actions our daughter revealed she was emotionally disturbed.

So many prayers were uttered on her behalf ... and ours.

Psalm 121:1 reminded me: "I lift my eyes to the hills. From where does my help come?" The psalmist answered his own question: "My help comes from the Lord, who made heaven and earth."

Psalm 121 is one of fifteen Songs of Ascent. These songs were sung by Hebrew pilgrims as they "ascended" the hills surrounding Jerusalem and climbed the steps to the temple, the dwelling place of the Lord. Some travelers may have been anxious about bandits potentially lurking in the hills. Others probably sang with joy, confident in the help always available from "the Maker of heaven and earth."

But everyone knew the origin of their help.

My help, too, came from the Lord.

A close friend referred me to a mutual acquaintance with two adopted daughters. She struggled with many of the same issues and shared information leading us to helpful specialists.

Realizing others struggled in anxious, painful silence with their emotionally disturbed children, I felt prompted to share our story.

But could I summon the courage to write our embarrassing story, to speak of our experience? Aloud?

I lifted my eyes—and my heart—to the Lord in prayer. He helped me. He gave me His peace and the courage to write, speak, and share a difficult, sometimes humiliating story; a story that might encourage someone else.

The Lord will give you the courage to share, too.

Debbie Lowe is a blogger, speaker, and writer. Her desire is to encourage women to wholeheartedly trust God in every area of their lives. Visit her at DebbieLowe.org and on her Facebook page, Debbie Lowe Life Lessons.

Feeding Hungry Souls

Brenna Kate Simonds

But Jesus replied, "You feed them!"
Luke 9:13 TLB

While preparing for the 2020 Tokyo Olympics, weightlifter Hidilyn Diaz from the Philippines found herself stuck in Malaysia for five months. With her home training plans completely uprooted, she built a gym and trained with jugs of water.

In her competition category, women lift above and beyond 200 kg—440 lb. A gallon jug of water weighs approximately 8.34 lb, or 3.75 kg. Now, that's a lot of water jugs!

Faced with so little to train with, most of us would have given up.

In Luke 9, Jesus presents the disciples with a similar challenge. The crowds were following Jesus, listening to Him teach, and hoping for healing. On this particular day, as it was late and the people were hungry, the disciples told Jesus to send them away, so they could find food.

Jesus' reply? "You feed them!"

The disciples were quick to say that all they had was five loaves and two fishes, adding "or are you expecting us to go and buy enough for this whole mob?" (Luke 9:13).

I often wonder, *What do I have to offer this world?* My heart is too quick to focus on what little I have rather than what God is able to do with my *little*.

I became a writer by accident. I wrote some mediocre research papers and tried my hand at fiction when I was younger. I quickly learned fiction is not a genre at which I excel!

In 2007, a friend asked if I would consider writing a few topical articles for an online publication, based on some life-controlling issues with which I wrestled. I thought, Way to jump right into the deep end! Not only was I unsure that my writing would be any good, but did I really want to talk about such personal topics?

Three initial contracted articles became eleven. I started getting feedback from people deeply impacted by the way I wrote. The more personal stories I shared, (I wrote about losing our second child to miscarriage), the more people responded.

What we have on hand might seem like it couldn't possibly be enough.

David's smooth stones.

Jael's tent peg.

The widow's jar of oil.

A boy's lunch.

Or some jugs of water.

Because of her creativity and perseverance, weightlifter Hidilyn Diaz won the Philippines' first Olympic gold medal in history.

All I had on hand was a journey God carried me through, a journey of learning to walk in freedom. It didn't seem like a lot, but in God's economy, it was enough.

Are we asking God to send *someone* else, *something* else, or are we willing to offer Him what little we have? Because with His help, it might just be enough.

———————

Brenna Kate Simonds is a writer of words and songs, a wife, mom, and missionary. She is the passionate about Jesus, is the author of "Learning to Walk in Freedom" and can be found at LivingUnveiled.com

Courage in the Storm

Nancy Smith

*This hope we have as an anchor of the soul, a hope both sure
and steadfast and one which enters within the veil.*
Hebrews 6:19 NASB1995

I'm not sure showing a film clip from *The Perfect Storm* was the wisest choice for a cruise ship audience. Especially as it showed the very scene where the fishing vessel, the *Andrea Gail*, was atop the highest wave imaginable for a split second before that wave fully engulfed her.

But then the Christian speaker explained that one thing everyone needs in order to survive the storms of life is enough "ballast" on board. Ballast is the heavy weight placed in the bottom of ships to provide stability and improve floating capability. Likewise, we need to take in God's Word daily as ballast to keep us balanced and prepared for the unexpected storms of life.

While we were cruising, my mother had been at our house watching our two boys. Within one hour of our coming home, I found her collapsed on the bathroom floor, prompting a call for an ambulance. She had suffered a massive brain hemorrhage.

The next day we stood by her hospital bedside to say goodbye as we watched her pass into eternity. The whole family knew Mom was going to be with her Lord because of the solid foundation of faith she and my father had laid.

My husband and I, exhausted and with our hearts breaking, wondered how we would be able to make all the necessary arrangements for my mom. But, because we had just spent a week praying, worshipping, and seeking God that "ballast" carried us through. Dad, though assured of the reality of heaven, was too shocked to help much. There were many details to attend to, but

God gave me the courage to write Mom's eulogy and speak at her funeral. Our daughter took a train home from college to give tribute also.

This is our blessed legacy of faith—our hope is in heaven because of Jesus' sacrificial love.

When circumstances become confusing and overwhelming, God is there. I know He guards my heart and directs my steps. Sometimes He will calm the storm, but other times He calms my soul and gives me the courage to do the next thing.

As a writer and speaker, I am compelled to share my stories because of God's continual love and faithfulness. My hope is in an unfailing God who is Sovereign and in control even when my life seems to be out of balance. My anchor is held by the promises in His Word and not by the empty promises of a broken world.

Has God called you to use your gifts, abilities, and share your stories? If you, like me, desire for others to find hope in the only "true Anchor" for their souls, join me in finding the courage to write.

Nancy Smith has a passion for sharing God's Word and encouraging others to grow through their own storms of life. She is also involved in disability and marriage ministry. Nancy loves a good cup of coffee and lives in Stoughton, MA. SecurelyAnchored.net

Using Your Voice for God's Glory

Rebecca Brown

Be anxious for nothing, but in everything by prayer and supplication, with thanksgiving, let your requests be made known to God; and the peace of God, which surpasses all understanding, will guard your hearts and minds through Christ Jesus.
Philippians 4:6-7 NKJV

With sweaty palms, a racing heart, and jittery nerves she put pen to paper, but to no avail. *Who do I think I am? No one will ever read this; and even if they do, they won't like it. Sally Sue's work is so much more flowery than mine; and every time Jenny posts, she gets millions of comments.* Her lament was palpable and stifling. No creativity would flow.

Deflated, she brought her anxious thoughts before the Lord. She thanked Him for giving her the ability to write. She chose to trust Him with her insecurities.

Later that day as friends came for lunch, she put out a lovely fruit basket for them to enjoy. As she watched each one make their different choices, God spoke to her heart. "My child," He said, "each of you has different tastes and different needs depending on the day or stage of life you've come to. Some desire the taste of sweet oranges or mangoes, others want the crunch of a tart Granny Smith, while others need something soft and easy like bananas or raspberries. I have given you a unique voice which speaks to one of these tastes. If you fail to contribute, someone's need won't be met. If there are only banana-type writers, who will fill the need of those requiring Granny Smith-writing?"

Please know, dear one, how vital your authorship is. Instead of comparing, let us celebrate each voice so that, as a whole, a bountiful cornucopia can be presented to meet the needs of all.

Come to the Father without anxiety, and trust in the One who loves you deeply. Know that He is enough for you. He is the One to please, and no one else. Ask Him for inspiration and insight. Then thank Him for how He is teaching you and how this understanding can be useful to others. When your trust is fully in Him, He pours over you a peace that makes no sense—even in the midst of your torment. Rest in that peace as He uses it to guard your heart and mind from any insecurity, hurt, or rejection.

And so, the writer reflects and begins her story again.

With sweaty palms, a racing heart, and jittery nerves she put pen to paper. With courage in her heart and peace in her soul, she wrote using her beautiful voice for the needs of those who required her unique writing. She wrote for the glory of her God, no one else.

Rebecca Brown is a chef, health coach, and author. She owns a health coaching business, teaches "eating for wellness" through lectures, coffee chats, and cooking classes. She lives in Connecticut with her husband. They have three children, and three grandchildren.

Venturing Out

Susan Call

When I am afraid, I put my trust in you.
Psalm 56:3

Will's face lit up in anticipation as the boathouse and dock came into view. Bright yellow kayaks lined one side of the dock while larger silver canoes flanked the other. The vast shimmering lake beckoned his five-year-old curiosity, sense of wonder, and adventure.

"Not so fast," his mom said, pointing to the life vests as they passed the racks by the dock, stopping Will in his tracks.

"Why do I need one of those?" he inquired wondering if he needed what appeared to be a less than attractive fashion accessory. His analytical mind wasted no time dissecting his mom's reply. *If* something were to happen out on the water, he would need to trust the life vest to keep him afloat.

Without missing a beat, he turned and pointed over to the swimming area. "Could I try it over there?" His logic was sound. If the vest allowed him to float in the shallow waters, he could trust it in the middle of the lake where the waters were murky and deep.

A few moments later Will waded cautiously into the swimming area, life vest firmly strapped on. Once waist deep, he leaned forward tentatively and allowed his feet to lift off the sandy bottom. A grin washed across his face as he realized the vest worked. He was floating without any effort of his own. Knowing he could trust the vest to carry him in shallow waters, he was ready to take a chance and venture out into the deep.

As writers, God calls us to leave the safety of shallow waters to go where we can have a greater impact for Him on the world around us.

If we attempt to set out on our own, we can find ourselves quickly over our heads and threatening to be sunk by an industry that often comes with rejection as a norm. We find ourselves fighting with our internal voices that can fuel our doubts that God has called us to write.

In such times, I take time to journal and remember the ways God has been faithful to show up, answer prayers, and open doors in the past.

Perhaps there is something to be learned from young Will. Quiet your doubt as you trust Him, lean on Him, and allow Him to be your life vest as you venture out into deeper waters as a writer.

Susan Call is an author, speaker, coach, and jewelry designer whose passion is equipping others to shake limiting beliefs, take their next step, embrace their potential, increasing their positive impact on the world around them. SusanCall.com

Staying Close to God

Patricia Frost

I wait for the Lord, my whole being waits,
and in his word I put my hope.
Psalm 130:5

"God is so good, He's so good to me," Sadie sang with gusto; and she meant it.

Smiling, we returned to our Bible study, but within ten minutes a lovely chorus spilled forth from the same sweet voice. Over time this became the norm. While the rest of our group shared Bible verses or insightful thoughts, Sadie shared music.

This got me thinking as well as digging through dusty boxes in my attic.

Years before, I had written a poem about a musician for my husband. After reading it he smiled and said, "That's nice." Although he seemed totally underwhelmed by my words, I thought the poem might just bless this lovely lady who couldn't stop singing. So, I carefully prepared a gift.

The old poem looked rather attractive in its new frame. Sadie read it and tears gushed from her eyes. "Yesterday," she confessed, "I vowed I wasn't going to sing at Bible study anymore. I scolded myself for not knowing a lot of Bible verses or deep thoughts. I felt rather stupid just singing so I said, 'I'll just keep quiet.'"

But then she read the beginning of my old poem:

> She cannot be silent,
> she cannot be still,
> created for music, created to fill
> God's holy purpose of worship …

My words affirmed to Sadie how much her songs delighted God and blessed the rest of us. Although written many years before, the poem found its perfect place and moment in time that morning. Sadie was overwhelmed and I was too!

A few years later my husband died. Anguish and sorrow poured out through my pen filling page after page of notebooks. For me, writing became a source of healing.

One morning I felt a nudge. Perhaps others could benefit from my words as Sadie had.

Glancing at my many journals, and prompted by Mark 11:13, I thought, "You've got a lot of leaves on your fig tree but not any real fruit." So, I began to write more intentionally. Could I possibly even write a book? Me—a low-tech redneck whose only technical skill came from a typing class fifty years prior?

God's Word encouraged me. From the story of Abraham I read, "I being in the way, the Lord led me" (Genesis 24:27 KJV).

As I stayed close to God (in the way) I became persuaded that He could take my experiences and translate them into words that would bless others.

I struggled to be a good steward of those words. The next few years became a season of seeking Him, writing daily, and worshiping as I waited.

Finally, my book was published, *A Widow's Offering.*" I was so excited! I shouted, "Woohoo, I've got a fig!"

Sadie was right. "God is so good, He's so good to me."

Patricia Frost, author of "A Widow's Offering," lives in a quiet corner of Connecticut. She enjoys good stories, good home cooking, and the good earth to dig in. Above all she loves encountering the Spirit of God in her quiet and not so quiet times. Contact her at JustPattyFrost@gmail.com

Count It All Joy!

Deb Haggerty

Count it all joy, my brothers, when you meet trials of various kinds, for you know that the testing of your faith produces steadfastness. And let steadfastness have its full effect, that you may be perfect and complete, lacking in nothing.
James 1:2-4 ESV

Count it all joy! How I laughed when I read those words. Count it all joy?

You have to be kidding. How can there be joy in my son being killed in an auto accident? How can there be joy when my mom keeps falling and lives in severe pain? How can there be joy when I have no purpose—wasting all the experience I'd gained over the past years?

Then God spoke to me in my spirit. "Sometimes, I call my kids home early to prevent a worse situation from occurring. And did not this experience, heartbreaking as it was, draw you and your husband closer together—taking the fallow years and bringing forth togetherness?

And your mom is here with Me and your dad and the rest of her family—she's totally without pain and very happy. And look how much joy you had caring for her—even those very late nights when you listened to make sure she was safe. Look how much you accomplished for Me during those hours with your prayers.

And consider the gift I gave you in your publishing company. You've been able to use all those experiences and talents I gave you in service to Me and to your authors and editors. You've followed the mission I gave you to come alongside others and work with them to get the words I gave them out to the public in the most professional manner possible. And, Deb, those words have not come back void. You won't know how many people have been impacted by the books you've published until you get home to Me."

And I realized I had been counting it all joy—the trials I'd faced had produced steadfastness—and that I lacked for nothing.

The years of wait indeed had weight. Though it was not readily apparent to me while I was living through them, it is very evident now that I am looking back.

I learned for myself the lesson I'd taught in a Bible study almost twenty years ago.

Take the Scripture words "count it all joy" and
- week one, emphasize *count*,
- week two the word *it*,
- week three *all*,
- and week four *joy*.
- Say the phrase daily and meditate on the emphasized word.

You will find you do count it all joy by month's end.

I am reminded of the many counted cross-stitch pictures my mom made for me over the years—exceptionally beautiful from the front, not so much so from the back. We may not see the joy as we're enduring the trials of life, but if we hold these verses tight in our hearts, we will rejoice in the finished picture.

In all things—count it all joy!

Deb Haggerty runs Elk Lake Publishing and encourages those authors and editors the Lord brings her way. She and her husband, Roy, wrote "Experiencing God's Love in a Broken World." Deb's memoir is "These Are the Days of My Life."

Writing Truth Seasoned with Grace

Rachael M. Colby

Therefore, my dear brothers and sisters, stand firm. Let nothing move you. Always give yourselves fully to the work of the Lord, because you know that your labor in the Lord is not in vain.
1 Corinthians 15:58

My editor politely declined to read my article because the preacher I featured didn't support his chosen lifestyle.

I cared deeply about my editor and agonized over how to communicate with him. "It distresses me," I wrote in the piece he refused to read but allowed to publish, "that some don't understand, it is possible to disagree with people's lifestyles and still love them."

A year later, I wrote another article. In this one, I featured interviews with ministers who addressed several hot-button issues. One pastor voiced his thoughts and God's word about the controversial topic—the one I had covered in my previous article, and my editor held a different opinion on.

Some suggested I not submit this latest article. I enjoyed a good relationship with my editor, and I didn't want to jeopardize the opportunity to share the Gospel that writing for this general market publication offered.

But God led me to weave my thoughts alongside my interviewees' and include the words I'd written for my editor the year before.

I wrestled with omitting the portion which showcased the pastor's controversial message, as others said I should.

But, No. And neither would I ask the pastor to alter his words.

"Thy will, Lord."

Courage is not an emotion. It's an action. Nor does it mean the absence of fear. It is a decision to stand for truth—even when afraid.

"If the choice is to appease man or please God, I must choose to please God," I texted a friend.

The phone rang.

"Hello! I've read and re-read your article," my non-religious editor said. "Well done."

He shared the impact of my interviewees' insights recorded in the 4,000-word article. "But," he said, "I thought the most powerful were these words of yours." And he read me the words he didn't know I'd written for him a year before:

Because we love people, we cannot support behavior we believe harmful to them. Because we love God, we strive to be faithful to His word and will for our lives.

I wept in gratitude to Jesus for giving me His strength to stand.

Courage for the Christian has nothing to do with comfort or convenience, but a faithful obedience to God's call and word. He undergirds as we obey—and how and when He uses our words is up to Him.

The Bible says faith without works is dead (James 2:17). Let us walk and write the works He's called us to.

Lord, strengthen me to stand, obey Your word and call, and exercise the courage to write truth seasoned with grace, humility, and love. Amen.

Jamaican born award-winning writer Rachael M. Colby resides in Cape Cod, Massachusetts. Wife, mom, beach bum, artist, Rachael writes to inspire faith, connect culture's questions with Christianity's answers, and uplift those who serve in tough places. Find her at TattooItOnYourHeart.com

Your Place at the Table

Kate Breckinridge

My Father's house has many rooms; if that were not so, would I have told you that I am going there to prepare a place for you? And if I go and prepare a place for you, I will come back and take you to be with me that you also may be where I am.

John 14:2-3

My husband and I switched our toddler between one another's arms as we took turns sweeping, vacuuming, and dusting. We played happy music over the speakers and threw jokes back and forth. We could hardly wait for our friends to come to our home that evening.

Hours later, with our daughter asleep in her crib and the house looking spotless, we cheerfully waited. But no one came.

I reflect on the verses above and wonder if Jesus has that same sense of sadness about His people. Jesus is not fragile or breakable, but He has lived a human life and experienced the entire range of human emotions. He can sympathize with my husband and me about our empty house since He's been preparing a place for His own guests for *eternity*.

He's laid out my place card before my seat at the dinner table, arranged the cushions in the coziest corner of the sofa, even set aside a special room just for me. But what if I don't show up? He waits, cheerful and expectant, and my place remains empty.

I know Jesus was talking about an eternal home when He spoke of "preparing a place," yet I can't help but think about how He waits for us here and now. He asks us to use our God-given gifts and talents to honor His Father and give Him glory, yet we often choose to not show up.

As writers, we are called to speak God's truth with pen and keyboard, paper and screens. When we don't use our gifts, we are ignoring the place that Jesus has set specifically for each of us to fill. When we settle for lesser things and place them over Jesus' calling in our lives, we are missing out on something incredible.

Jesus says, in John 14:4, that we know the way to the place where He is going. How often do I take that path? How many times do I choose a detour that serves myself or allows distractions into my journey, instead of moving toward Jesus and fulfilling His dreams for my life?

Jesus wants us where He is. He wants us closer than close because He loves us. He has prepared a place for each of us, and He tells us over and over that He is with us, He will not forsake us, and He will lead us Home. *What would happen if we each believed those truths?*

We would pull up chairs, take our places at the table, and watch something amazing happen in Jesus' presence.

Kate Breckinridge is a native Southerner who made New England her home in 2014. She spends her time writing, baking, being the Church right where she is, and having adventures with her husband, daughters, and fluffy Goldendoodle. KBreckinridge.wordpress.com

God's Call to Write

Rachel Paukett

Some trust in chariots and some in horses,
but we trust in the name of the LORD our God.
Psalm 20:7

Words swirled throughout my mind. *You can't write, you have no training. No one will want to read your work. You can't make a living that way.*

These were some of the voices filling my head after hearing God's call to write the autumn of my senior year of college.

I have always enjoyed creating stories. Even as a child I thought up tales as I drifted off to sleep, stringing together an epic stretching across many nights. I worked on a book throughout my college years, as a break from long hours of homework and studying. But, as almost an adult, nearing the end of many semesters of hard work to earn a degree for a good solid future, writing never figured into my long-term plans.

God's call emerged wild and exciting, frightening and unknown. Everyone would think I was crazy. I thought of myself like Noah, building an ark with no water in sight.

Despite knowing God had called me to be a writer, the voices of doubt and logic assailed me as I tried to *figure out my next steps*. Focusing on what the world found rational—"chariots and horses"—only fueled these voices. But when focusing on God's voice and trusting Him, I found the courage to follow my calling.

While the world focuses on the tried-and-true and what makes sense, our God is not confined by these constructs.

Dwelling outside of time and beyond the limits of human understanding, He calls us to be our best and truest selves. Sometimes His call leads to places we would never have considered, *if*

He had not spoken into our lives. Family, friends, and strangers alike may believe our calling is foolishness, but we can trust in the Lord our God.

Despite all my doubts, I put my trust in God and His calling to write.

I joined groups of fellow writers who have taught me and encouraged me. I even completed a "very rough" draft of the story I tinkered with throughout college.

The "chariots and horses" of this world may seem like a safer path to take, but by having confidence in God and continuing to write I have found immense joy in pursuing His calling. You can too.

———————

Rachel Paukett has been writing and creating stories since she was young. She enjoys writing fiction and is working toward her goal of finishing a book. Rachel has an article published in Bella Grace Magazine and an academic journal.

Finding a Way to Do It

Catrina Welch

For God is working in you, giving you the desire
and the power to do what pleases him.
Philippians 2:13 NLT

With the announcement of the pregnancy, came an introduction to the mom—not exactly how I dreamt of becoming a grandma. Still, the news came with a renewed hope that perhaps this baby would be a wake-up call for my son and end my nightmare.

It didn't.

My hope plummeted as the dysfunctional pregnancy developed and the baby arrived. "Grandmother" quickly became "guardian" and before long, I was responsible for protecting the newborn from all the hurt and frustrations that addiction brings into a family.

In the midst of it all, I neglected to guard my own heart.

Baby Laneigh was left in our custody only weeks before our last child would go to college and, honestly, I wasn't too excited about having an egg tossed into our empty nest.

Sleep deprivation certainly influenced my emotional state. But it was the parents' head-games, court cases, visitations, and interventions that consumed my heart and diminished my hope of ever having time to write again.

I was worn out and bitter. As a non-fiction writer whose main message is "overcoming Confidence Conflicts," I'd forgotten my own advice. How could I write about "Confident Beauty" when I was consumed with the ugly?

I couldn't.

In fact, I didn't find the courage to write again until I let go of my resentment.

Once I submitted my circumstances to God and gave up my victim-mentality, He was able to work in me. Suddenly I had a renewed desire and a fresh power to do what pleased Him. Now, instead of focusing on the distractions that continue to rob my time, I look for mini moments to put pen to paper; and God has granted me not only the ability to focus with a toddler underfoot, but the love of this opportunity to raise such a beautiful little girl.

It pleases God when we act according to His good purpose for us.

If we know we are called to write, then we need to find a way to do it. Yes, there are major setbacks and messy circumstances that deserve our time and attention, but our God is bigger than our challenges and He can equip us to do what He designed us to do.

If you, too, are struggling with giving writing a priority, I encourage you to guard your heart with all diligence. Heed the Apostle Paul's advice to the Philippians because your words shine God's Light in this dark world.

"Do everything without complaining and arguing, so that no one can criticize you. Live clean, innocent lives as children of God, shining like bright lights in a world full of crooked and perverse people" (Philippians 2:14-15 NLT).

Catrina Welch is an author, speaker, and life-coach. She helps women and children overcome Confidence Conflicts—especially Image Issues through Supreme MakeOver events. She and her husband are raising Laneigh on Cape Cod. Find her at CatrinaWelch.com

Relying on God's Strength

Lorri Dudley

The righteous will flourish like a palm tree ...
Psalm 92:12

Danger, plot twists, and reversals. We love them in movies and books. They are what keeps us glued to the screen and page and heighten our adrenaline. The tension keeps us watching the next scene and reading that extra chapter, even though we should have turned off the light and gone to bed an hour ago.

While it's great to have conflict in a drama or novel, most of us prefer a peaceful, stress-free existence. Do we have it? No. Jesus states in John 16:33, "In this life you will have trouble..." Not may or might, but we *will* have trouble.

So, when problems arise how do we keep them from shaking our very core?

We must face storms like the palm tree.

Whereas the oak tree is known as mighty, strength is not enough to face fierce wind and high water. When a hurricane comes, the oak can be uprooted, or its branches broken. However, the palm tree has different qualities. It is flexible. It bends but doesn't break. It folds its fronds so that the wind passes through and doesn't tear the tree apart. The palm also spreads its roots, more wide than deep, giving it a sturdier base.

The palm tree doesn't thrive by avoiding storms. It is uniquely designed to survive tropical hurricanes.

Psalm 92:12 says, "The righteous will flourish like a palm tree."

In harsh climates, we can stay fresh and green, and still bear fruit in old age. We can stand tall as a testimony, proclaiming that the Lord is our foundation (Psalm 92:14-15).

As the palm bends, we also need to bend our knees. As the palm folds its leaves, we too need to fold our hands, take heart, and cry out to the One who has overcome the world. When life's hurricanes sweep through our lives, we don't rely on our own strength. We will not be overwhelmed and sink into despair. We stay rooted in the One who not only saves and sustains us but will help us flourish in adversity.

Be like the palm tree. Draw from the true source of our strength, God Almighty.

———————

Lorri Dudley, author of the historical romance "Leeward Island Series," lives in Ashland, Massachusetts with her husband and three teenage sons, where writing romance allows her an escape from her testosterone-filled household. LorriDudley.com

Receiving the Breath of Life

Shawn Parisi

Indeed, we felt we had received the sentence of death.
But this happened that we might not rely on ourselves
but on God, who raises the dead.
2 Corinthians 1:9

Do you feel discouraged, beat down, as if there is no way your situation will ever change?

This was exactly how Paul felt when he wrote his letter to the Corinthians. The situation was so dire that he and his companions thought it was a death sentence.

A death sentence brings you to the end of your hope. The initial shock may make you numb, sad, angry, helpless and out of control, or overcome with grief regarding the loss of future dreams. Paul describes it so well, "We were under great pressure, far beyond our ability to endure, so that we despaired of life itself" (2 Corinthians 1:8). It was as if it hurt him to even take a breath.

Have you ever been in this place? Have you felt like, *if the Lord himself does not breathe life into these lungs I will not be able to take another breath?*

What are we to do in such times? How do we begin to navigate such a feeling?

Learning to live is not just "hanging in there." It's grasping hold of what God has called us to in that day and running after it. When we choose to follow God, He writes our story and we can move from a death sentence to deliverance.

Living with congestive heart failure has been one of the greatest difficulties and blessings of my life.

In the early days of my shock and disbelief at this diagnosis, I was angry, scared, and confused—unable to take a breath. I thought I had received a death sentence. However, recognizing God as the Author of every chapter, of every day of my life has allowed me to receive His breath of life.

I have experienced the same truth as Paul when he says, "this happened that we might not rely on ourselves but on God who raises the dead." When we become Christ followers, we no longer need to fear death. We don't ever have to face a death sentence as we are *alive* in Christ. It's not that we don't question, *how did this become my life?* The beauty is that we don't have to be angry, scared, or confused.

Oh friend, you don't have to live in despair, because the Author of the greatest story ever told is also the Author of your life.

Have you been given a "death sentence?" Are you having trouble breathing? Who will be the author of *your* story? Allow the One who breathes life into you, to write it.

Shawn Parisi is a native California girl who has learned to love her New England home. She spent her career in sales and twenty years in youth ministry. Shawn has been blessed to teach both women and youth the beauty of God's Word.

A Greater Plan for Your Words

Konnie Viner

When anxiety was great within me,
your consolation brought me joy.
Psalm 94:19

It was the phone call everyone dreads. "Our mother is being rushed to the hospital," my sister in Kansas blurted out.

Anxiety quickly became "great within me"—frantic concern about whether I would make it in time. I got an early flight the next morning and joined Mom in the Intensive Care Unit that afternoon.

The diagnosis was a bleeding abdominal ulcer. We were told she had received the maximum number of transfusions, and nothing could be done to save her life. Surrounded by her children, several grandchildren, and great grands, she took her last breath the next day and painlessly joined my father in heaven.

Just a few hours earlier, Mom had joyfully sung hymns with us and recited Psalm 23 and other favorite verses from memory. She had taught us how to live well; now she showed us how to die peacefully and without fear.

My first novel was nearly finished, but I had not told Mom about it because I had based one key character on her—the protagonist's godly mentor—and I planned on dedicating the book to her as a surprise.

When I returned home a few days after the funeral, I struggled to continue writing. Words didn't flow onto the page. I had lost my passion for the story, and I questioned if I could even finish the book. Dealing with grief and the shock of her sudden death, I knew I was slipping into depression.

I questioned why God had given me the story and the character modeled after Mom's personality, wisdom, and faith. I felt the character had died also, no longer existing because Mom had gone. I lost the joy of writing the mentor's words which reflected Mom.

Setting my manuscript aside, I asked God whether I should abandon the story.

He began to quietly reassure me that the story needed to be finished—it could bring encouragement through the wisdom and faith of the mentor's character.

Women need mentors and many do not have anyone in their lives who fulfill that role.

I slowly began writing again, working through tears. As I finished writing, I wished Mom could have read the book and known I created the mentor in her honor.

Instead of dedicating the novel, *Amaryllis Journey*, to Mom, it was dedicated to "the memory of" my godly mother and mentor, Betty Louella. To my amazement, *Amaryllis Journey* received the Golden Scroll Fiction Book of the Year Award. Many women have commented how blessed they have been by the character of the mentor.

I love that Mom lives on in the pages of my first book, due to God's greater plan.

God had gently removed my anxiety and replaced it with courage. His consolation brought joy to my soul and, gratefully, to many readers as well.

Where you feel stalled in your writing, for whatever reason, God has a greater plan for your words, too.

Konnie Viner writes to encourage women with the assurance of God's love and faithfulness in the midst of brokenness and disappointment. She is the author of "Blueberry Bungalow," "Amaryllis Journey," and "Rested Soul Resilient Heart." KonnieViner.com

When God's Call is Scary

Janet Fisher Aronson

For the Spirit God gave us does not make us timid,
but gives us power, love and self-discipline.
2 Timothy 1:7

Timidity? Do people even use that word anymore? I prefer the word *reluctant*. I'm not so much fearful or timid as I am reluctant to do what God has created me to do.

When it comes to writing, I came kicking and screaming into the arena. After all, I wasn't a writer, I was a musician, a voice major. All I wanted to do was sing songs that other people had written. I've often said, "Set it to music and I'll do the rest." But write? Why would God ask me to do that?

2 Timothy 1:7 became my life verse when I was a camp counselor in the early 1980's. I was a very new believer and felt so far behind all the others there, even the kids. What did I know about the Bible, about Jesus? How could God use me to minister to these kids who had known the Bible from childhood?

God has a marvelous sense of humor, doesn't he? He stepped right in, and this Bible verse became a topic for all of us at the camp. For the leaders, because we needed to be bold and courageous in our interactions with the kids. But also, for the kids who needed to know that life would be scary at times, yet God had given them power to get through even the toughest days.

Scary! That's the word I use when thinking about being a writer. After all, hadn't an English teacher told me to stick with music? Hadn't a college professor written all over an essay, making me believe that I didn't have writing in my wheelhouse?

106

An alternative translation of this verse says, "for God did not give us a spirit of fear." In the Bible, we are told not to fear 365 times! How about that for a reminder!

As I've grown in Christ, I have recognized that when God calls us, He equips us to do what He asks. He's given us the power to move forward, putting all His love into us so that we can be the person He created us to be. Then, by His Spirit, He has given us the self-discipline to sit down and write.

Don't have the words? Pray for the Spirit to guide you. Don't have self-discipline? Pray again.

God didn't call you to write because you have it all together. He called you to write because that was what He planned from His very first thought of you. And He will be with you all the way!

Janet Fisher Aronson is an author, speaker, and life coach. Her book, "Marking Time with Mark," was published in 2019. Janet is the Director of Discipleship at Easton Baptist Church in Easton, MA. Visit her website at JanetFisherAronson.com

Keep Moving Forward

Maureen Laub

And the LORD said to Moses, "Why do you cry to Me?
Tell the children of Israel to go forward. But lift your rod, and
stretch out your hand over the sea and divide it. And the children
of Israel shall go on dry ground through the midst of the sea.
Exodus 14:15-16 NKJV

As a nation, Australia believes in the philosophy of always moving forward. For this reason, the kangaroo and the emu were chosen as the national symbols for the Australian coat of arms. They are the only two indigenous animals to Australia that are incapable of walking backwards due to their inverted knees.

God commanded the Israelites, as His chosen people, to move forward. Their exodus from Egypt, out of bondage, and into the Promised Land was not just a physical journey, but an emotional journey of moving forward in trust as well. When fear got the better of them and the way ahead seemed impossible, Moses went to the Lord with their complaints. God's reply was essentially (my paraphrase), "You saw Me do one miracle after another in Egypt. I've led you thus far with abnormal and miraculous natural wonders, a cloud by day and a pillar of fire by night. Now, we come to this sea … a sea I created, and you're still afraid? Why are you crying to Me? Have faith. Go forward!"

However, God didn't stop there: "But lift your rod …"

Why did God tell Moses to lift his rod? God could have said, "Step back and watch!" Sometimes bold faith is enough. We only have to believe, and God will do the work. However, in certain situations God requires more of us—He asks for faith plus action.

Moses did exactly as God directed. Moses' faith and obedience through action resulted in one of the most famous events of divine deliverance in all of history. Not only did the sea part, but every drop of water in the sand at the bottom of the sea was squeezed out, leaving dry ground for the Israelites to walk on.

Is that scary blank page in front of you, your Red Sea? Do you sit and wonder, *How will I ever get to the other side? There is no way. I cannot do it!*

Have faith that the Lord has brought you to this place, and to this moment. Couple your faith with action, believe that the Lord has equipped you with the tools necessary to, "raise your rod," and walk forward like the Israelites, kangaroos, and emus to get the job done.

Maureen Laub is from Hollis, NH. She works for the US Air Force and has travelled to 36 countries. After seven years of divorce, she and her ex-husband remarried. She is mom to three teenagers, two golden retrievers, and three cats.

We Are in God's Hands

Lisa Larsen Hill

*Trust in the LORD with all your heart and lean not
on your own understanding; in all your ways
submit to him, and he will make your paths straight.*
Proverbs 3:5-6

We waited for my husband's biopsy results from the urologist. Was it cancer? If so, what stage? What would the treatment be? I had just been diagnosed with severe osteoporosis and we wondered how much more bad news we could take.

Scheduled to conduct our church service the next day, Roger and I rehearsed the Scripture about the woman who hemorrhaged for years. Being members of the Network of Biblical Story Tellers, we *tell* the scripture instead of reading it, bringing a new light to the stories. But, surrounded by fear, I wondered if I would be able to speak without breaking down.

Later, when alone, I sensed God's voice, "Are you listening to what you're preaching tomorrow?" (My message focused on the woman's trust to be healed.) Further, I heard, "Have you had troubles, challenges in your past that you thought you'd never survive? How did you get to here? I was with you then and will be with you always." The voice stopped, leaving me with hard memories. All that worrying for naught. The Lord had carried me when I walked through my valleys and gave me life again with both a loving husband and a call to write. So, why did I doubt?

Through tears and a smile, I recalled my word for the year. Trust. And my verse, Proverbs 3:6 (TLV), "In all ways acknowledge Him and He will make your path straight."

With fresh insight, I understood why the words *do not fear* are in the Bible 365 times, one for each day of the year. Do worries stand in the way of writing or speaking the words God has put in your heart? Do you have memories of the valleys you survived when God sustained you?

Our Lord wants us to live life and live it abundantly. We are in God's hands, and we will be all right.

Memorizing Bible verses reminds me of Who is in charge of my life. Perhaps it can for you, too.

Attending writer retreats and conferences and joining a critique group has introduced me to amazing mentors and learned writers. I count my blessings for the women of faith and hope who richly enlarge my family circle. Being part of a faith writers' community surrounds us with a "cloud of witnesses" to sustain, inspire, commiserate, teach, and be there in times of need. It can do the same for you.

May you view your life experiences knowing the Lord was, and is, with you every step of your journey. He says, "Do not be anxious how you are to speak or what you are to say, for what you are to say will be given to you in that hour; for it is not you who speak, but the Spirit of your Father speaking through you" (Mathew 10:20 RSV).

Lisa Larsen Hill is pursuing publishing for her completed biblical fiction. She is CEO (Chief Enthusiastic Officer) of Seeds of Faith for Women: SeedsOfFaith4Women.org. A certified lay speaker, she enjoys telling biblical stories and sharing the message of God.

Showing Up as Our True Selves

Kathy Kim

*For we are his workmanship, created in Christ Jesus
for good works, which God prepared beforehand,
that we should walk in them.*

Ephesians 2:10 RSV

I have learned there is nothing more powerful than discovering who I really am.

Such revelation can be a humble acceptance of the way we have been created. It is agreeing, surrendering, and aligning ourselves to who we already are in Christ.

Genuine wholeness is coming to an understanding of who God says we are and living in the light of that truth. As we recognize Christ's sacrifice for us on the cross, we become bold and courageous in our life's journeys to becoming whole in mind, body, and soul. We truly become fearless and unapologetic to who God says we are. We do not show up to please others. We do not seek approval from others. Being who God created us to be is absolutely freeing.

For me, this topic of wholeness has been transformative. In my own spiritual journey, I have learned to graciously receive and embrace all that God has revealed to me.

I am a working mother juggling many responsibilities and wearing different hats on any given day. I used to divide my life into compartments—a mother, career woman, ministry leader, pastor's wife, and more. In each of these roles, I often tried to fit into a mold I created based upon the expectations of others.

I felt unable to show up authentically as myself and pursue my passions in each of these different areas of my life.

In particular, I made plans to walk away from my corporate job, which had become a daily grind, in order to pursue my passions. But God challenged me in my quiet moments and showed me I could be myself *and* pursue my passions in the marketplace where He has placed me. My work is now meaningful. I have begun to add value and impact others by serving them in the same way I do at home and in ministry. I have stopped straddling two different worlds, which often left me conflicted. I have learned to be confident in who God created me to be in every area of my life. The journey to wholeness is an opportunity to experience what God has already established within you.

Are you ready to view where God has placed you and where God wants you to be? God has given you gifts and He desires you to use them to your highest potential by showing up powerfully as your true self.

His grace allows you to pursue wholeness in your head, your heart, your mind, and your entire being. This process is called sanctification—becoming more and more like Jesus Christ.

Would you take a moment to think about your journey to living fully as a believer? Where might God be asking you to authentically align yourself to God's will in every area of your life? Meditate on Ephesians 2:10 where God tells us that we are the work of His hands, His masterpiece made to bring Him glory.

I encourage you to embark on your journey to deeper life in Christ—there are many companions along the way!

Kathy Kim is the mother of three school-age kids and is married to Peter, the senior pastor at Trinity Covenant Church in Manchester, CT. She serves in women's ministry. Her passion is to encourage and mentor women. Kathy is a project manager in the pharmaceutical industry.

A Calling to Victory

Yvonne Ortega

"For I know the plans I have for you," declares the Lord, *"*
plans to prosper you and not to harm you,
plans to give you hope and a future."
Jeremiah 29:11

Twenty years after my divorce, I sensed God wanted me to write about the hard topic of divorce among Christians.

My response? *Lord, take me home early or bring on the rapture!*

While struggling with the difficult topic of divorce, I focus on Jeremiah 29:11 where God used the Babylonian captivity to crush the pride, rebellion, and materialism of His beloved children. As I write about divorce among Christians, God also crushes my pride, rebellion, and materialism.

And yet, this same verse also promises "hope and a future." Like God taught His beloved children, He teaches me about the eternal value of obedience and trust in Him without grumbling, doubt, or hesitation. He also teaches me about gratitude.

I thank my heavenly Father in advance for a future with Him as I bravely begin to write my book about divorce among Christians.

As I write, I refuse to become distracted by anything the enemy sends my way. For instance, recently, my friend tested my computer speakers and found a blown right speaker. She said, "The other speaker can go next. Order both at once and make an appointment with my technician."

Her technician installed both computer speakers and indeed found a swollen battery on the verge of an explosion sooner rather than later. He replaced it when he installed the new speakers. He told me, "The explosion could have caused you blindness, deafness, or both."

My choice to act now to prevent a future blowout saved me from a potentially worse fate.

Those computer issues and the restoration of my health from gas poisoning three years ago cannot deter me from the courage to complete my book. Neither can the recent malfunctioning of my microwave oven and stove. Instead, they offer me an opportunity to walk with Jesus Christ, to submit to the Father as Christ did, and leave an eternal legacy.

I embrace the courage to write about divorce because God will give me far more than I can imagine now and the prosperity of an eternal home with Him. I call that a double victory.

What will you write about with courage? Where is God calling you to victory despite obstacles trying to deter you?

––––––––––––

Multi-interviewed, author of the "Moving from Broken to Beautiful" Book Series, Yvonne Ortega helps women find peace, power, and purpose through God's Word even when they feel overpowered. She celebrates life at the beach where she walks and builds sandcastles. YvonneOrtega.com

Is Writing a Gift?

Carla B. Howard

Be strong and take heart, all you who hope in the LORD.
Psalm 31:24

Do you know what your gifts are? The Bible mentions spiritual gifts in both Romans 12:6-8 and 1 Corinthians 12:8-10. These gifts are specifically given to believers to help us fulfill our purposes on this earth in Christ. God also gives us the gifts of individual talents that will work toward serving the same purpose.

The question is, Do we have the courage to use those talents and glorify Him? Even more, Do we have the courage to admit we have a talent for writing and that the Lord Himself has gifted us with it? For what a responsibility that is! And what courage it takes.

As a budding writer, I am still questioning whether I have been given this talent.

The little writing that I have done thus far has been for the library where I work, appearing in a column in the free town paper. Every time I submit a column, the questions *"Do I have what it takes?"* and *"Will anybody read or like my work?"* haunt me. All this angst for a free paper!

I pray before, during, and after submission. For even though the subjects are secular, as a Christian my words need to glorify God, or at the very least not offend Him. Herein lies the responsibility for this gift.

Another trap I fall into is hiding behind the excuse of busyness and just living life. I will always "get around to" writing when I finish school, this project, or when my daughter is grown up. Talking with a published friend after an inspiring writer's conference, I asked her how she did it … raising two children, working, running a household, *and* writing?

Her answer was simple: She always kept a journal handy and in between all the "busyness" of life, she would jot down ideas. Then, when the children were in bed, she had a "writing time," and used those ideas captured during a busy day to begin creating. What a way to honor God, His gifts, and to use one's talent!

Writing takes courage, and, if we are hoping in the Lord, we are commanded to be strong and take heart in whatever it is that we do. If writing is that "whatever we do," then we need to go about it purposefully and wholeheartedly.

When fear and insecurity threaten to overshadow the words we are writing and keep the ideas from flowing, let's turn to the One who made the words and is "able to do exceedingly abundantly above all that we ask or think" (Ephesians 3:20 NKJV).

With His guidance, we can celebrate both having a gift for writing and being courageous enough to use it, as God has commanded us.

———————

Carla B. Howard is a librarian and makes her home in Canton, MA, with her husband Tim, daughter Jackie, and sister Melissa. The three are entertained daily by two cats, Shawn and Gus, and a beautiful rescue dog named Bella.

Where to Seek Shelter

Tammy Sue Willey

He will cover you with his feathers. He will shelter you with his wings. His faithful promises are your armor and protection.
Psalm 91:4 NLT

As a little girl, this motto was beaten into me: *Life is tough out there and my job is to toughen you up.*

I can't say I embraced the belt or back-hand of my dad's parenting skills. However, they are what shaped my view of me and life. My survival skills were carefully honed work-a-rounds, sharpened by a heavy hand.

Today, I thank God for the guidance of His hand.

Are there days when you are tired, hurried, misunderstood? Are you grieving loss after loss? Work layoffs, infertility, vehicle repairs, a leaky roof, an incomplete list that never ends?

Do you tell yourself, *You're stupid and can't make anything work?*

On those days, stop, breathe, and pray so you aren't confused about whose voice you hear. "Don't worry about anything; pray about everything … His peace will guard your hearts and mind …" (Philippians 4:6-7 NLT).

It has taken a lifetime for me to learn to rest in the shelter of the gentle voice of my heavenly Father:

"Let me tell you, sweet thing, I see amazing growth since you've chosen to walk with Me and break from old familial patterns which no longer serve you. It takes courage to walk away from shaming insults. I can't help but smile and think, 'There goes my fabulous daughter, just as I designed her!'

Don't lose heart in these dark days clamoring to pull you backwards. I see the temptation you are up against as the world's voices pour lies over you: being a good employee seems irrelevant, your story doesn't matter, your views are wrong and you need to apologize for things you didn't do, or worse, apologize for the way I created you.

Remember you are my handiwork, created in my Son, Christ Jesus, '... to do good works ...' (Ephesians 2:10). Being bombarded by lies isn't easy, but if you hang with me, I'll help you through.

Keep your heart on Me today, not on back-then. Yes, life is tough out there, but I'm not toughening you up. I am offering you shelter. I am holding back countless obstacles being hurled at you from the enemy. I don't break little girls' toys, call them fat, or drag them down the stairs to build their character. These things grieve my heart. Your character continues to grow as you persevere with Me, running your race—even writing your hard, hard story for all the world to read.

My precious one, cling to Me and My promises, for I will always hold you up and never tear you down."

Courage is knowing your voice, standing strong in God's truth, and remembering where to seek shelter. Are you ready to share your hard, hard story?

Tammy Sue Willey's memoir "Wounded Song", journeys through her father's anger and her mother's silence in an abusive childhood. Her question became, "Now What?" Travel with her on her path to forgiveness and restored relationships. TenderRestoration.com

Shout It from the Rooftops!

Jill Robinson

What I tell you in the dark, speak in the daylight;
what is whispered in your ear, proclaim from the roofs.
Matthew 10:27

Sometimes, as God's messengers we can be reluctant, weak, or even maybe stubborn. Yet, God has not changed his mind about using His children to reveal Himself to those who don't know Him.

When we decide to believe in the Lord Jesus Christ, one of the awesome opportunities we have is to be His mouthpiece, His hands, His feet, and His heart.

For someone, we may be the only "Bible" that person will ever read. So many people in the world don't know the goodness and loving-kindness of God, or His many other great attributes. His good intentions, plans of hope and a future for their lives are also unknown to them.

As Christians, we should solemnly take on the responsibility of being empowered by the Holy Spirit to help bridge this gap between our inadequacies and God's mission for our lives. Despite feeling unqualified, we can achieve the end goal to make Christ known.

In addition to being Jesus' hands and feet through random acts of kindness and generosity, we use our words to be His mouthpiece. We share God's amazing works in our own lives—how He heals us, transforms our character, gives us wisdom to engage with the pragmatic side of living, helps us deal with relationships, and how He longs to be involved in even the minute details of our lives.

"What I tell you in the dark, speak in the daylight; what is whispered in your ear, proclaim from the roofs," Matthew 10:27 tells us clearly. The polarity between "whisper" and "proclaim" is worth noting. And the use of the word "roof" should not be taken for granted. "Roof" can be any means that will allow the Gospel to be proclaimed. Rooftops were greatly used in Jesus' time and standing on the roof meant that many people could hear your message.

Let's use our words to reach people we will never meet; in places we will never go. Your words will be like a hot cup of tea to a cold, lonely soul. Proclaiming God's goodness and hope from your rooftop, will be Christ's whisper in somebody else's ear—maybe a pivotal message spoken at a crossroads in their faith journey, or a tiny tweak that makes them finally believe that God is indeed good, that He is real, and His promises are true.

Jill Robinson was born in the Philippines where she worked as a high school English teacher and a press relations officer to a congressman. She moved to the USA to join her husband, became a mother to two boys and started taking care of a farm. She documents life through her blog and is working on a non-fiction book. JillRendonRobinson. blogpsot.com

Tell of His Glory

Katy Lee

*The twenty-four elders fall down before Him who sits on
the throne and worship Him who lives forever and ever, and cast
their crowns before the throne, saying: "You are worthy,
O Lord, To receive glory and honor and power; For You created
all things, And by Your will they exist and were created."*
Revelation 4:10-11 NKJV

I believe that God is forming an army and his scribes are
his recruiters.

His weapon of choice is the pen, as the Bible proves it is
more powerful than any double-edged sword. As the Author of
Life, God knows that writing is not an easy task, and it will take
a courage that many lack. It will take a perseverance that many
can't withstand. Badges of honor go out to a select few for a
reason. But He has chosen you, and it is not His will for anyone
to perish.

For that reason, we as writers must pick up our swords
and write.

We read in Revelation that the enemy is defeated by the
blood of the Lamb and the word of our testimony. No matter
what God has called you to write, whether fiction or nonfiction,
an article or a podcast, your testimony is woven through every
sentence and paragraph, and it has power. Every word is gold,
as it speaks to all God has done for you and through you. Your
every word does battle for His glory.

When we write for Him, our words become crowns of gold
that we lay at His feet, a demonstration of thanksgiving and
honor for all He has done for us. To put the pen down and keep
His blessings locked up inside, would be equivalent to putting

our sword down on the battlefield and letting the enemy defeat us. We must do everything we can to not trade our badges of courage for white flags of surrender. We must tell our stories, defeat the enemy, and crown the Lord with many crowns.

Believers are promised crowns of various sorts. Crowns of rejoicing, crowns of righteousness, and if we endure, we will receive the crown of life and the crown of glory. These crowns will last for eternity. But when we stand in victory, we will willingly cast our "crowns" at His feet as an act of worship.

Our writing is one of those acts of worship—our accomplishments performed in service of His army. As we write, we can crown Him King of every area of our lives, testifying to His goodness through our words. So, I encourage you to pick up your swords and lay down your crowns.

Your testimonies, your accomplishments, and all the words of gold will tell of His glory and point others to Him.

Katy Lee is a best-selling and award-winning author of inspirational romance, suspense and mysteries. She splits her time between the valleys of Connecticut and the Rocky Mountains of northern Utah. Her websites are KatyLeeBooks.com and YourNovelCompass.com

Afraid? Write Anyway

Jeanne Doyon

All believers, come here and listen,
let me tell you what God did for me.
Psalm 66:16 MSG

I can relate to the Lion in *The Wizard of Oz*. He was afraid of his own shadow. Scary unknowns made him run away rather than face his fear.

When I began my writing and speaking journey, I was like the Cowardly Lion. I wrote pages and pages, hiding them because of fear. I struggled with the what ifs. What if it's no good? What if I'm no good? Not to mention, the apprehension of baring my soul to the world with my words.

I tried to muster up courage but didn't take a first step until someone encouraged me with some tough words. "Shame on you for hiding your gift!" she said, handing me the phone number for an upcoming writer's workshop.

I discovered that overcoming fear required me taking a first step.

I made the call. I sent writing samples. And I received an invitation to the week-long workshop. Once on site, I figuratively wrung my tail like the Cowardly Lion, sure that I didn't belong there until the director spoke. She announced we were there because we had a gift. I sobbed.

As a new writer, I struggled with self-doubt and comparison—sometimes I still do. That was why it was essential to join the writing community; to both learn the craft and discover how to tell my story.

Opening up about my struggles became another fearful step in my journey. It meant uncovering the roots of my fear and insecurities and being willing to share them.

Sharing was a scary hurdle for me. However, the chains that had bound me since childhood began to break and the pieces that were formerly buried started fitting together until I saw an emerging picture. As God loosened those roots, I could see where my shame and people-pleasing began. The more I was set free, the easier it became to share my testimony. The more I shared my story, the more His glory peeked through the cracks of this broken vessel.

In Scripture, those who encountered Jesus were given stories to tell. And because they were brave enough to share, lives were changed around them. God in His infinite knowing, puts "brave" back into our souls so we can be witnesses of His faithfulness.

If you are like me, you will face many first steps and hurdles that fear will try to control. Be brave. Keep going. Your story matters. It has the power to encourage others.

Because of Jesus, God has given you a story to tell. When fear starts to squash your courage, remember He promises to walk with you—every step—over every fearful hurdle. So instead of wringing your tail, you can proclaim His change in you.

Jeanne Doyon writes and speaks from the heart, connecting Scripture to everyday life. She leads the Pausing for R & R Retreat for women. She is available to speak at women's events. Discover her blog, The Stream's Edge, at JeanneDoyon.com

Writing Without Shame

Renee Story

Instead of shame you will have a double portion.
Isaiah 61:1-7

I t's difficult for shame and courage to coexist.

While we don't always recognize shame on its own, it can be hidden in seemingly good things like purpose which puts our souls on a self-focused relief-seeking expedition. No matter what form it's in, shame keeps us in the dark, maybe even preventing things like blessing, joy, and freedom. It can be all-consuming and, if left unchecked, can steal from us the beauty of life and faith.

We can ask ourselves: Is shame preventing us from living and sharing our authentic life story?

If we don't want shame to have power over us, we need to sift through our fears to not only recognize shame but to confront it. But managing shame in what we do, think, and say, leaves no room for rest. Managing our shame quickly becomes one more thing we can't seem to do, which brings more shame, continuing the cycle.

How do we stop the cycle? We start pursuing healing.

There was no shame in the garden until Adam and Eve tasted the fruit God told them not to eat. Adam said the first shame-filled words when he spoke from his shrubbery hiding place, "I was naked" (Genesis 3:10).

While Adam and Eve's decisions in the garden opened the door for shame, Jesus opened the door for our healing. While we still struggle, Jesus enables us to live in the inheritance of freedom from such things as shame. When we wonder if we will ever come out from under the heavy blanket that informs so much of our reactions and decisions, Jesus allows the fullness of walking in obedience with courage.

With Jesus, we find healing. True, deep healing.

Healing is offered by Jesus as the remedy for shame's evil grip on our hearts and minds. It is the great exchange that has been paid for—for you, for me. When we give Him all of our shame, He gives His peace.

Instead of trying to manage the shame in your life, you can believe the truth: You are loved and accepted right where you are. Doesn't that sound wonderful? As you begin walking *without* shame as your constant companion, you will get a fresh look at who you were created to be.

Perhaps you, like me, were created to be a hope-giving communicator of the good news of Jesus. As God renews your mind, helping you believe the truth He says about you, then you will discover the courage to be who God designed you to be as a hope-giving communicator.

Renee Story is a worship leader and a Restoring the Foundations minister in Connecticut. Her passion is to see individuals healed, empowered, and on mission, a true reflection of freedom in Christ. Discover more at AnchorAndKey.org

When We Feel Like We're Not Enough

Susan Case

"I tell you the truth," Jesus said, "this poor widow has given more than all the rest of them. For they have given a tiny part of their surplus, but she, poor as she is, has given everything she has."
Luke 21:3-4 NLT

Years ago, I belonged to a singing group that performed in our community. One weekend, we sang for a local nursing home. To be honest, it wasn't one of my favorite gigs. Some of residents would fall asleep during the performance, and it was kind of depressing seeing the condition of many of the patients.

However, that weekend, I met Annie. Annie, in her mid-forties, had cerebral palsy. She welcomed us with delight. We enjoyed talking with such an enthusiastic audience member, even though Annie's unclear speech made her difficult to understand.

By request, we sang a medley of hymns and Annie joined in, singing loudly. We found this a bit distracting. Any resemblance to the melody was purely coincidental, and she sounded in pain. Yet Annie's face shone with pure bliss. She was rejoicing in her Savior, and it suddenly struck me how beautiful her song must be to Jesus.

I try to remember Annie's wholehearted offering of praise when I'm feeling not enough. It's easy to doubt my gifting and minimize the value of the opportunities I'm given. After all, my songs and dramas will probably never be heard outside my home church. What difference could my meager offerings make in God's kingdom?

But Scripture tells us to be faithful with what we are given, even if it doesn't seem like much. The servants in Matthew 25 who were given five bags of gold and two bags of gold were praised that their investments rendered more.

The Apostle Paul rejoiced in his weakness, because he knew it made God's power "all the more" visible (2 Corinthians 12:9).

The widow's two measly coins didn't seem like much compared to the larger contributions of the rich and powerful. Yet because she gave all she had; her offering was of more value in God' economy (Luke 21.3-4).

Everything we have and everything we are comes from God, and He wants us to use it for His glory. We don't need to be afraid that we're not enough because frankly, we aren't. But God is.

Thank you, Lord, for the abilities and opportunities you give us. Help us to be fearless and faithful to use our gifts as you direct, and to trust you with the result. Amen.

Susan Case served for nearly 40 years in her local church as a worship leader and scriptwriter. Most recently, she made a major career change to become a registered nurse. She remains open to where God leads her next.

The Blessing We Offer Others

Cathy Gohlke

Blessed be the God and Father of our Lord Jesus Christ,
the Father of mercies and God of all comfort,
who comforts us in all our affliction, so that we may be
able to comfort those who are in any affliction, with the comfort
with which we ourselves are comforted by God.

Corinthians 1: 3-4 ESV

O ur lives are kaleidoscopes of experience and roller coasters of emotion—years of adventure, days of turmoil, moments of sweet peace. Our heights, our depths, the in between, are all colored through relationships with others living out their own kaleidoscopes of experience and roller coasters of emotion.

It is that universality of experience that connects us with readers, that understanding of everchanging realities and emotions that binds us together, helping us sympathize and empathize with our brothers and sisters on life's journeys.

We write creative stories using what we know, what we've experienced, observed or researched, and what we've seen reflected in the eyes of others.

While it's true that "there is nothing new under the sun," we each uniquely experience and respond to life's trials, losses, and difficulties. Mercifully, we don't experience or respond to these alone. Because we've surrendered our lives to Him, our Lord walks beside us, the Holy Spirit fills, guides and comforts us, and our Heavenly Father shelters us through storms.

Our lives provide gold mines of inspiration for us as writers.

By mining and writing of both the hard places and the comfort we've received, not only do we glean more from our experiences, but depth and emotions blossom through our characters, enabling them to live and breathe on the page.

We needn't detail our journeys through cancer, abuse, or the tragic loss of a loved one—but we can infuse our characters and their journeys with details we know, emotions we've experienced. Anger, pain, disillusionment, doubt are all part of life ... but for followers of Jesus so are comfort, peace, enlightenment, and hope. Our journeys—the lives we've lived, the lessons we've learned, and the comfort and healing we've received—provide vital resource material for the stories God has uniquely prepared and gifted us to write, for the blessings He's prepared us to offer others.

Lord, thank You for the gifts of experience, for the heights and depths we've known, for the comfort we've freely received and for all You teach us day-by-day as we yield ourselves to You. We long to use these life gifts for good, for Your glory, and the benefit of others. Enable us to share the bounty we've received through our pens, infused by Your Spirit. Through Jesus Christ our Lord, Amen.

Cathy Gohlke is the bestselling, Christy Hall of Fame, Carol and INSPY Award-winning author of ten critically acclaimed novels. Request a virtual book club visit or subscribe to her newsletter at CathyGohlke.com. Follow her on Bookbub and Goodreads.

But God

Lucinda Secrest McDowell

My flesh and my heart may fail, but God
is the strength of my heart and my portion forever.
Psalm 73.26

I gulped and inwardly berated myself. Yet again I had allowed someone's words to wound my heart and crush my spirit:

"We love your writing, but your social media platform is too limited."

"We're going to pass on this project and go with something similar from a fresh voice."

"Your book is beautiful and profound, but too spiritual for our audience."

In such moments the voices of those who graciously invested in my words through fifteen published books and countless speaking events somehow faded into whispers. And I found it hard to recall the encouraging messages from people who had reached out to thank me for sharing stories that touched their lives.

Because, upon hearing those words, "my flesh and my heart" *failed.*

You too? Perhaps when you accepted that guest blog assignment or signed that contract, you were filled with both daring and delight at such an adventure in creating a message to help and heal.

But today you stare at a blank screen. Doubt and despair bring on the inner critic. *Who was I to think I could write on such a complex subject?* or *What will people think if I vulnerably share my hard story?*

I'm with you. Been there, done that. So, after forty years as a writer/speaker, I have the gift of two important words for both of us today.

"But God."

- Can you even imagine how many times I've felt like giving up? "But God ..."
- What about when I wanted to disappear, feeling unworthy and irrelevant as a colleague shared her stellar achievements? "But God ..."
- Or those occasional moments of emptiness, weakness, or discouragement—when no words would come? "But God ..."

"*But God* is the strength of my heart and my portion forever." (Emphasis mine.)

God's sovereign intervention in my life and work give me courage to keep following my call to write words of truth and grace, while releasing the way in which He will use them. His unconditional love gives me courage to ignore the voices of comparison and competition, focusing on my own unique gifts and opportunities.

I think back to others whose lives were changed by those two words—"But God."

David ran from Saul's evil pursuit into the wilderness ... "but God did not give him into his hand" (1 Samuel 23:14).

Joseph's jealous brothers sold him into slavery in Egypt ... "but God was with him" (Acts 7:9).

I don't know where you need courage today, but I know from Whom you will find it—if you will but open your hands to both release and receive God's strength and power.

Lucinda Secrest McDowell is a storyteller and seasoned mentor who loves "Helping You Choose a Life of Serenity & Strength." A graduate of Gordon-Conwell Theological Seminary, she is the award-winning author of 15 books including "Soul Strong" and "Life-Giving Choices." She wrangles words at LucindaSecrestMcDowell.com

reNEW – spiritual retreat for writers & speakers

... renewed in knowledge after the image of him.
Colossians 3.10 (KJV)

reNEW is a community where you can find godly encouragement for your writing and speaking journey. We are open to all beginner and seasoned writers and speakers who desire to communicate the good news of Jesus through their written or spoken words.

At reNEW, we believe the core of our calling as writers and speakers is faithfulness to Christ. And so, our emphasis is on the need to grow deep inwardly, so we can be effective in our outward reach.

Our community exists that you might renew your:

- Faith in Christ and commitment to deep spiritual growth "after the image of Him."
- Vision for sharing your unique story and message through writing and/or speaking.
- Relationships to receive and give encouragement to others in this creative community.
- Craft and skill in all areas of communication by being "renewed in knowledge."
- Soul, through a deliberate time of retreating from ordinary life.
- Courage to share your words of hope with a broken world.

Our reNEW retreats focus on:

- Relaxing atmosphere in a refreshing environment conducive to thinking, writing, praying, studying, and listening to God.
- Dedicated space and time for writing, research, or tweaking your work in progress.
- Teaching and leadership from professional faculty who are dedicated to Christ and willing to share their journeys.
- Celebration of each victory and acceptance of all on the path.

- Fellowship around tables, walks, and spontaneous interaction with a variety of people who are seeking to live authentically.
- Opportunities for growth and learning through a variety of teaching presentations.
- Worship and prayer times that focus on Almighty God.
- Support and sharing of ideas, lessons learned, and practical help to increase the depth and breadth of your reach.

Writing is often a solitary experience and reNEW desires to continue to invigorate our existing community and to enfold others into our celebration and support. We hope you will pray and plan now to join us on this journey.

Keep up with our latest events and news at reNEWwriting.com

Facebook @Renew – spiritual retreat for writers & speakers
Instagram @reNEWwriting
Email info@reNEWwriting.com

Mailing address: reNEW, P.O. Box 290707, Wethersfield CT 06129

Made in the USA
Middletown, DE
09 July 2022